WHEN
BUYERS
SAY
NO

Other books by Tom Hopkins

How to Master the Art of Selling
The Official Guide to Success
Mastering the Art of Selling Real Estate
Low Profile Selling
Sell It Today, Sell It Now, co-authored by Pat Leiby
The Certifiable Salesperson, co-authored by Laura Laaman
Selling for Dummies
Sales Prospecting for Dummies
Sales Closing for Dummies
How to Master the Art of Selling Financial Services
Selling in Tough Times

Other books by Ben Katt

Joyful Relationships
The Power of Persuasive Preaching

WHEN BUYERS SAY NO

ESSENTIAL STRATEGIES FOR KEEPING A SALE MOVING FORWARD

TOM HOPKINS *and* BEN KATT

BUSINESS
PLUS

NEW YORK   BOSTON

Business Plus
Hachette Book Group
237 Park Avenue
New York, NY 10017

www.HachetteBookGroup.com

Printed in the United States of America

RRD-C

First Edition: April 2014

10 9 8 7 6 5 4 3 2 1

Business Plus is an imprint of Grand Central Publishing.
The Business Plus name and logo are trademarks of Hachette Book Group, Inc.

The Hachette Speakers Bureau provides a wide range of authors for speaking events. To find out more, go to www.hachettespeakersbureau.com or call (866) 376-6591.

The publisher is not responsible for websites (or their content) that are not owned by the publisher.

Library of Congress Cataloging-in-Publication Data
Hopkins, Tom.
    When buyers say no : essential strategies for keeping a sale moving forward / Tom Hopkins and Ben Katt. — First edition.
        pages cm
    Includes index.
    ISBN 978-1-4555-5059-3 (hardcover)—ISBN 978-1-4555-5058-6 (ebook)—ISBN 978-1-4789-2698-6 (audiobook)   1. Selling.   2. Persuasion (Psychology)
I. Katt, Ben J.   II. Title.
    HF5438.25.H6667 2014
    658.85—dc23

2013038655

Tom Hopkins

*To my beautiful and loving wife, Michele,
who said yes to sharing her life with me.*

Ben Katt

*To Kristina, my dear wife, who faithfully
stands by her sales man.*

Acknowledgments

The authors would both like to acknowledge and thank Judy Slack, Vice President of Business Development for Tom Hopkins International, Inc. for her role in keeping the communication flowing between all parties involved, coordinating the workflow, and copyediting the original draft of this manuscript.

Special thanks, also, to the legions of sales professionals around the world who allow us to continue to practice our craft. Thank you for constantly challenging us to come up with new ways to help you do the job of serving your clients well.

Contents

Contents

SECTION 4
The Buyer Said Yes

Introduction:
What You Can Expect to Gain
from This Book

You won't win every potential sales opportunity. Even the highest-income-earning sales professionals in your industry walk away empty-handed at times. It's simply the nature of the business. Once you readily admit that, you'll stop looking for the magic bullet for closing every sale. Then you'll be in the right frame of mind to learn strategies that can help you win *more* sales than ever before—including those where the buyer says *no*, not once but multiple times.

Selling is a game—a sport—where the players prepare, do the best possible job they know how to do in the field, and take home the trophy of a closed transaction frequently enough to satisfy their drives for success and desires for accomplishment. However, when people don't win often enough, they leave the field of selling—some battered and broken. The truth is that selling can be a brutal sport when you take it on without knowing the rules and nuances of the game.

The goal of this book is to help you sell victoriously more often than you do now. On the one hand, these pages will delve deeply into the nuances of presenting products and services to potential clients. On the other hand, you'll discover how to quickly step away from the game in order to keep your mental bearings in the sales process—and then never lose control of a selling situation again.

In short, this is a book of strategy. You'll learn how to use a sales compass that's called the Circle of Persuasion. With it, at any given moment during the sales process, you'll be clear about the next step you need to take to stay on the path to a closed transaction. You'll also be able to make the right choice when a buyer presents you with the inevitable—and often unexpected—fork in the road to a closed sale.

This book will not cover where and how to find new business or how to gain confirmed meetings with buyers. It won't provide you with any follow-up strategies, either. It is totally focused on the actual sales presentation, from the moment you begin to establish rapport to when your buyer gives you the final *yes*.

Always know that there can be any number of reasons why buyers initially say *no* to your offering. What you do when you hear them say it will make a world of difference in your level of success. In fact, when you learn how to use the strategies in this book, you'll actually look forward to hearing the word *no*, not just once but several times in the selling process, because you'll know exactly what each *no* means and what you should do or say next.

Too often, salespeople allow selling situations to become uncomfortable when a buyer is resistant or hesitant. They start to feel rejected or defeated. They mentally pack away their sales materials and start thinking about the next appointment. Unfortunately, those defeatist thoughts and feelings show in their demeanor and attitude, and the entire sales process comes to a screeching halt. The average salesperson ends up leaving those selling situations with his head down and his tail between his legs, after making a farewell request to the buyer for permission to stay in touch.

"Keeping in touch" is certainly better than being told never to contact the buyer again. However, just imagine how the average salesperson's life would be different if, when he heard the buyer say *no*, he employed tactics to build a bridge straight back into the sale and another opportunity to ask for the business—with no uncomfortable pauses, no pushy or aggressive moves, no manipulative maneuvers. *It can be done.*

The answer lies in these pages. It's been proven successful by thousands of sales professionals who have already learned and employed the strategies here, and it all starts with the Circle of Persuasion.

In fact, the sales process can and should continue after the buyer initially says *no*. And it quite often leads to yet another *no*. However, when properly handled, even a half-dozen *no*s from a potential client can be redirected and converted to a *yes* without causing harm to the relationship that's being forged.

When you learn how to properly reengage a potential client after the initial *no*, you'll gain real confidence, and that confidence will show in your demeanor—winning over more clients than you have been doing thus far in your career.

This is not a book about theory. It is an instruction manual. Read these pages with a highlighter, notebook, and pen. Give serious thought to how you can incorporate these strategies into your daily selling scenarios. Practice the nuances contained here and then reap the rewards of a prosperous and fulfilling sales career.

Tom Hopkins
Ben Katt
Fall 2013

SECTION 1

—

The Buyer Says No

1. The Buyer Said No

"Well, Jim, that new equipment you showed me sure is nice, but unfortunately I'm just going to have to say no."

"We appreciate all the information you've shared with us, Mary, but we're not going to do this right now."

Those are typical words and phrases salespeople hear all day long, every selling day. For average salespeople those words signal defeat. The gut reaction experienced when hearing them is an immediate one of failure and rejection—something salespeople go through on a regular basis.

In fact, since rejections are so common, it's a wonder that so few salespeople anticipate hearing them and prepare to deflect the negative feelings they can create. Most salespeople just accept those words and the feelings they generate as part of the selling game.

How often you hear the words and phrases above will depend on your abilities and skills as a salesperson. But what you do and say *after* hearing them will make a world of difference in your closing ratio and in your personal bottom line.

GETTING TO "YES"

This is a book about *yes*. But the starting point is *no*.

The truth of the matter in selling is that very few buyers will say *yes* the first time they're asked to own a product or service. Yet, the irony is that most salespeople are willing to give up and accept rejection after hearing that first *no*.

Think about how you feel, what you do, and what you say now when you read the words at the beginning of this chapter.

- Do you feel the physical effect of disappointment? It's that sinking, let-down feeling. It can be a tired feeling as your formerly pumped-up selling emotions trickle down the drain.
- Do you mentally stop closing and simply move into "Let's keep in touch" mode, where you decide what to leave behind and what to pack away, then focus on your next meeting?
- Do you say, *That's okay, I understand,* or *I'll touch back just in case you change your mind*?

That's how *average* salespeople respond. So the first question is, do you want to be average—or do you want to encourage yourself to become better than that?

TWO KEY POINTS TO BEAR IN MIND

The first point of this book is to convince you not to give up on the sale too soon. There's still a whole lot of selling left to do *after* you hear the word *no*.

The truth is most *nos* are not dead ends but simply forks in the road. As a sales professional, your job is to be well prepared to switch from your intended path to the sale to a new path that your buyer may choose for you. You must be flexible enough to keep the process moving toward your original destination. In short, the goal remains the same even though the route may change.

Think of the first *no* you hear (and possibly the first few *nos*) as nothing more than a potential detour. Believe that there's still a way to make the sale and that your well-trained mind will quickly seek out alternative routes or approaches—especially after you finish studying this book.

Typical buyers will say *no* as many as five times before saying *yes* to owning a product or service. Many salespeople, when they hear that statistic, think it means that to become a top salesperson, one must keep badgering buyers with the same information until they finally cave in.

In a supersimplified form, they imagine a conversation that goes something like this:

Salesperson: *"Would you like to buy?"*
Buyer: *"No."*
Salesperson: *"Are you sure? It's a really good deal."*
Buyer: *"No."*
Salesperson: *"We both know you have a need for it. And you told me you have room in your budget."*
Buyer: *"No."*
Salesperson: *"You can count on us to deliver what we promise. We advertise on all the major TV networks and have been around for one hundred years."*
Buyer: *"No."*
Salesperson: *"It includes free shipping and your choice of colors."*
Buyer: *"No."*
Salesperson: *"At this price, they won't last long. Now is the best time to buy."*
Buyer: *"Well...maybe I'll go ahead."*

This perception of selling situations explains why many salespeople shy away from persisting in their persuasion efforts when they first hear the word *no*. They don't want to be rude or aggressive, but they just don't know where to go with the conversation once the buyer says *no*.

The second point of this book is to help you understand that the successful persistence demonstrated by top performers doesn't involve rote repetitions of the same information.

Each *no* has a different meaning. Thus, each type of *no* requires a different approach.

Top-producing salespeople explore each sales scenario from all angles, testing each possibility until they find a win-win combination that works for the buyer and their company, or…they exhaust all the possibilities and leave the sales appointment with the satisfaction that they truly offered the buyer all the options available to meet her needs.

Their type of conversation is more likely to sound something like this:

Salesperson: *"Would you like to buy?"*
Buyer: *"No."*
Salesperson: *"You mentioned earlier that you were concerned about taking delivery before your busy season begins. If we could guarantee that you will receive the product before then, would that make it easier for you to move forward today?"*
Buyer: *"Well, that would help, but I think we'll still hold off."* (No)
Salesperson: *"You also showed interest in customizing our deluxe model to meet your specific needs. If I confirm in writing that we can deliver that customization, would you agree that added value would pay for itself during your busy season?"*
Buyer: *"Um, it probably would, but I'm not sure our people have the ability to maximize the features on your product."* (No)
Salesperson: *"I am so glad you brought that up. With the deluxe model, we include free video tutorials plus one year*

of online support. And I will personally meet with your team after delivery to address any issues that might arise. Do you feel that is adequate support to get your team up to speed?"

Buyer: *"Probably so... we just don't have it in the budget this year."* (No)

Salesperson: *"Funding is an important consideration. If we could work with you on a schedule for the investment, would that make a difference? For example, what if we were able to spread the investment out over time? What amount would you feel comfortable with as an initial investment?"*

Buyer: *"Hmm... I don't know. Let me think about it."* (No)

Salesperson: *"I understand. An important decision like this deserves some thought. Mr. Buyer, you've shown interest in the benefits of this product during our time together. You've mentioned how this product would increase your profits during your busy season by doing more [state the benefit] and [state the benefit]. What would need to happen for you to feel comfortable with moving ahead toward gaining those benefits today?"*

Buyer: (Extended silence) *"I guess I could put a down payment on the company credit card..."*

Five *no*s and a *yes*. Do you see the difference in tone between the two dialogues? In the second dialogue, each *no* was, in fact, not a dead end. Each *no* was actually a step closer to a *yes*, because the salesperson explored another dynamic required by the buyer to say *yes* today.

This is a book about *yes*—about closing more sales when you are confident your product will fulfill the buyer's needs. *No* is being explored in this first chapter, because that is the pivotal point in the sales presentation where the salesperson either continues on toward a *yes*—or simply gives up and ends the sales appointment.

The word *no* is a guidepost—not a stop sign!

If you let your spirits sag at the first *no*, it'll show in your demeanor. One of the most important truths about persuasion is that you keep few secrets from your buyers. In other words,

- If you don't like sales, your buyers will know it.
- If you don't believe in the value of your product or service, your buyers will know it.
- If you don't like something about your buyers, they will know it.

If you have indeed given up on the sale, your buyer will sense that you've given up. If someone asked the buyer later how he knew you had given up on the sale, he probably couldn't say why. But the reason is that you nonverbally and subtly communicated that message to your buyer through your facial expressions, posture, and gestures. That—and starting to pack up your presentation materials!

As a result of your nonverbal communication, your buyer loses interest. Why would a buyer lose interest when you give up on a sale? Buyers like to buy from confident people. Confident salespeople continue exploring all the options after they hear the word *no*. That negative word doesn't faze them at all.

Besides, if you no longer believe you can make this sale, you are, in essence, saying your product or service is not the best for your buyer. You'll soon be on your way to meet with other potential clients, with nothing to show for your time spent with the buyer who might have made a purchase if you hadn't given up. In other words, **when you give up, all you've accomplished is to warm these buyers up to making a purchase from the next salesperson who comes along.**

Handling *no* is not a test of wills where you have to steel yourself to accept the *no*s in selling as challenges to be endured. Effectively handling *no* is a matter of preparation, perspective, and attitude. Top sales professionals rise to meet the challenges that accompany each *no* and keep potential sales alive.

If *nos* weren't a natural part of the selling process, there would be no need for salespeople.

EXPAND THE POSSIBILITIES

Why don't more salespeople follow a line of questioning like the one illustrated in the second dialogue above? One reason is that many salespeople are not aware of the full range of actions they can take when buyers say *no*. This book will teach you how to expand the number of possibilities you have at your command.

What is the result of having a full box of sales tools to employ when buyers say *no*?

1. You will be more relaxed and satisfied with your selling career.
2. Your buyers will like you more. And that's vitally important.

As you will learn in chapter 6, the deeper the rapport you maintain with your buyers, the more they will trust what you say and the longer they will continue to explore the possibilities of buying from you after they initially "pass" on your product or service.

Here's a simple example of continuing the sale after hearing *no* that you've probably encountered hundreds of times: Imagine you're in a restaurant. As the server starts to clear away your dinner dishes, he asks if you've saved room for dessert. Reflexively, you say *No, thank you*, don't you? A good server won't let that be your final answer. He'll smile and go on to describe in great detail the freshly baked apple pie with the superflaky crust, the ice cream sundae with strawberries that were picked just this morning, and the seven-layer Belgian chocolate cake with cream cheese icing.

What has he accomplished? He's kept your attention and kept your interest alive. Then he'll ask which would be your preference if you *were* going to have dessert.

Since his descriptions allowed you to mentally experience each of those desserts in your mind's eye (and possibly got your taste buds activated), you might ask how large a serving of the cake is. When you do, you've given the server an opportunity to expand upon the details, clarify your interests, and probably increase his tip, because you will start to think about sharing a dessert with someone else at your table although initially you were thinking that you had no room for dessert at all. You just want a "taste." You begin to rationalize digging into that dessert. The opportunity for the server to make a sale is still alive. He's more than ready and willing to present you with the dessert you've indicated would be your preference and to close that sale.

Hard to believe, but the concepts in this book really are that simple.

When you master the strategies of what to do and what to say when your buyer says *no*, you'll keep more of your opportunities to sell alive. And you'll complete the sale with a strong percentage of those opportunities while the average salespeople of the world will have given up and headed out the door.

CHAPTER 1 KEY POINTS

- What you do and say *after* hearing *no* will make a world of difference in your closing ratio and in your personal bottom line.
- Few buyers will say *yes* the first time they're asked to own a product or service.

- Most *no*s are not dead ends but simply forks in the road.
- Typical buyers will say *no* as many as five times before saying *yes* to owning a product or service.
- Each *no* has a different meaning. Thus, each requires a different approach.
- If you let your spirits sag at the first *no*, it'll show in your demeanor.
- When you give up, all you've accomplished is to warm the buyer up to making a purchase from the next salesperson who comes along.

2. What No Really Means

*N*o is one of the most powerful words in all the languages on the planet. It is the catalyst for hundreds of emotional reactions. It can make or break not only a sale, but a person's day, month, or year, as well as having a major impact on her life as a whole.

Here are just a few examples of the emotions people might experience depending on the meaning of the word *no*.

Relief: No, you do not have cancer.
Exhilaration: No, you did not fail the licensing exam this time.
Sadness: No, we won't be together for the holidays.
Happiness: No, we don't have to move away from the family in
order for me to take that better job.

Depending on the situation, some people experience tremendous fear when hearing it. In fact, the anticipation of hearing the word *no* can create so much anxiety in people that it can be harmful to their physical and mental health.

Fear is an especially strong reaction for those who are relatively new to the field of sales. Not knowing how to handle *no* in a selling situation keeps many salespeople from ever achieving greatness in their careers. For that reason alone, it's critically important to learn to anticipate hearing it as early in your career as possible. Then, you can prepare for what happens after the *no*.

Through education and preparation, you will learn how to turn *no*s into continuations of the sales process whether it's the sale of:

- a time to meet with potential clients,
- yourself, your company, your brand,
- your actual product or service, or
- getting clients to give you referrals.

Potential clients will respond to your requests in one of three ways most of the time: *Yes*, *No*, or *Maybe*. In selling, a *maybe* is to be treated as if it's a *no* until it can be turned into a definite *yes*. And a *yes* isn't truly a sale until buyers actually take the action step of:

1. giving you a check,
2. approving a credit card transaction, or
3. providing an authorization on a purchase order.

In other words, the buyer must take action in order for a sale to be completed.

Note: If your type of product sale requires multiple visits, the action you may need the buyer to take would be to confirm the next step in the sales process—possibly your next visit.

YES, NO, OR MAYBE

Can you think of any other responses? There are hundreds of variations of how buyers give those three answers, but those are the three basic responses you will hear when you ask buyers to take action. So if those are the only three responses, why would a salesperson become discouraged when hearing *no*? Certainly, it's more fun and profitable when buyers say *yes* right away, but if every buyer said *yes* right away, wouldn't companies simply hire order takers instead of salespeople?

As a salesperson, your job is a lot more complex than presenting products and taking orders. Your job is to act as both a detective and a consultant. The detective in you searches for clues as to what buyers really want to own. The consultant in you then guides them to reaching the same conclusion you did after understanding their needs—that your product is the right solution for them.

Here is a question for you to consider: why would anyone agree to meet with you and spend the time to listen to your presentation if they weren't interested in the benefits of owning your product or service? Do you listen to presentations from salespeople about products and services that you have no interest in? Of course you don't.

It's time to rethink the meaning of *no*.

RETHINKING THE MEANING OF "NO"

In the English language, the word *no* can carry many shades of meaning. It would be a financially costly mistake for you to assume that the meaning your buyers assign to the word *no* is the same as the meaning you assign to it. Some of the possible meanings of *no* are as follows:

1. <u>Lingering questions</u>: In sales, the word *no* very often means that the buyer hasn't had all of her questions or concerns addressed yet. Perhaps she's confused about how your product compares to the competition's. That's a challenge you must be prepared to address.

A confused mind says *no*. It's an instinctive, protective device of the human psyche. If the buyer doesn't see a clear way to go with regard to your product, he'll tend to put off making any kind of decision.

2. <u>Inadequate explanation of benefits</u>: If you've done your job of qualifying your buyer and are confident that your product will indeed serve her needs well, a *no* just means you haven't completed the client education process that's inherent in selling.

If this is the case, not providing enough information isn't necessarily a flaw in your presentation. Different buyers need different amounts of information delivered in different ways before considering a decision. Generally speaking, it's better to give too little information and have buyers ask for more (in this case, by saying *no*) than to give too much information and lose buyers on the basis of information overload or boredom.

Trust your instincts during your presentations and close when you feel the buyer has enough information to make an educated decision. If the buyer consistently asks for more information after your initial closing attempt, *then* it is time to make an adjustment in your presentation.

3. <u>Additional discovery is required</u>: A *no* may mean that you need to investigate further to determine what aspect of your presentation wasn't clear. Remember, a confused mind says *no*. Chapter 9 covers ways to be more direct and persuasive during your presentations.

4. <u>A misstep in qualification</u>: You may need to go back to the qualifying or needs-identification step in the sales process to be certain you are presenting the right product for the buyer's

situation. This scenario may be due to your missing something when you were identifying needs earlier in the sales appointment. It also may be due to a buyer being unclear as to her true needs.

Because your presentation was effective in educating the buyer on *what you incorrectly understood* to be the appropriate product or service, the buyer may say *no* to your initial offering. The buyer may not be aware that you carry another product that will meet her newly-realized needs. Only with further conversation can you discover this epiphany and then present the better product.

5. <u>Unrevealed questions/objections</u>: Perhaps the buyer hasn't told you everything yet about his circumstances as to needs and his ability to afford what you're offering. What? Don't buyers tell you everything up front that you need to know to offer a win-win opportunity and close the sale?

Sometimes this is merely an issue of trust. One of the most powerful times to build trust is after a buyer says *no*. As mentioned above, buyers are often unaware of their real objections and questions until they start to become educated about the products and services that provide solutions. Or, perhaps they like the product but not the financial terms you're offering. The point is that by using the proper selling skills, tools, and strategies in the correct manner, you can continue to move the sale forward despite initial reluctance from the buyer.

6. <u>Timing</u>: The buyer's *no* may just be a way of slowing the sales process down. It may mean "No, not right now." Good timing is important when *you* make purchases, so why wouldn't it be important to your buyers? By discussing options in timing, you may discover a time frame that is quite agreeable to your buyers even if it isn't today.

If you believe your buyers are saying "No, not right now," it may be because they thought of going ahead at a future date (or they could just be procrastinators). Your job is to find out when is the best time for them to become truly engaged, and determine if you can do anything to help them take advantage of your offer sooner rather than later.

You may say, "I understand you're hesitant, Sue. When do you think you'd like to start having greater peace of mind by owning a life insurance policy?" Or, "Sue, based on all the benefits we've discussed here tonight, when do you think you would want to take advantage of this program?" Sue may have a large bill due this week, or she may have a reimbursement check coming that she plans to use for this investment. The point is, you can't move the sale forward until you know what is truly holding her back.

7. <u>Features</u>: Their *no* may mean "No, not that size or color." When hearing those types of *no*s, well-trained salespeople will reflexively ask questions to clarify what the potential clients mean. You might say something like this: "I hear what you're saying, Bob. To help me understand a little bit better, what would I have to say or do to help you start taking advantage of the benefits of this new equipment that you seem to like so much?" Bob might jokingly come back with "You could tell me it's free." Then you know that the money is likely the issue. You then keep the sale moving forward by working on financial solutions for Bob.

8. <u>"No, not you"</u>: With some buyers, the *no* you hear could even mean "No, not you." Please realize that with some product sales the buyers aren't just buying the product—they're buying future involvement with you. In many cases, the salesperson becomes the key connection between buyers and the company, and the buyers may just not have been "sold" on you. They may not feel

comfortable with your ability to serve their needs. You always have to demonstrate your own level of competence as well as your product's benefits.

Remember, people prefer to do business with people they like. It's important to help the buyer like you and trust you so he'll listen to what you have to say, take your advice, and want to be involved with you in a long-term business relationship.

There are many reasons that potential clients may say *no*, but lack of interest is probably not one of them. Disinterested people won't waste their time meeting with salespeople and listening to presentations. So, when you have a buyer's attention, it's because she's truly interested in knowing if you, your company, and your product can resolve an issue or challenge she's having. Once again, the job falls to you to identify or discover what her needs and expectations are as they relate to your product or service.

You are the only one who can ultimately determine what each *no* means in every selling situation. You do that by keeping the conversation alive through the use of precisely crafted questions. By mining the information you need to know in order to determine if and how you can help the buyers, you'll close more sales that previously would have gone by the wayside.

YOUR REAL JOB

Let's get to the heart of the issue. Many salespeople think they are paid to give sales presentations. They mistakenly believe that the presentation is the single most important aspect of selling, and as a result they put all of their time and attention into giving it. They believe that with a little bit of small talk and one memorized way of presenting their product, they can build a sales career.

Granted, giving a good presentation is critical. But it's only one aspect of the sales process, and it needs to be flexible depending on the needs of the buyers. Unfortunately, few salespeople understand that showing off what their products can do is not really selling.

Presenting and then expecting the buyers to whip out their checkbooks, credit cards, or purchase orders has a name in the sales industry. It's called "wait-and-see selling." Salespeople who rely on that type of selling work harder and earn less money than those who are willing to invest time in developing their skills in the other steps of the sales process.

Wait-and-see selling does not address the unique needs of each buyer. Instead, it leaves the buyer feeling like she is hearing a stereotypical sales pitch. The salesperson throws the information at her. The buyer has to catch it and then sort it out to determine what's relevant to her. It's no wonder that so many buyers are resistant to sales efforts.

Those same unprepared salespeople give the reins of the sale to the buyer by never asking questions, never getting to know the individual buyer's needs, wants, fears, and desires. That's counterproductive.

In selling, the person asking the questions controls— and leads—the sale.

If the buyer takes the lead by asking questions, he could drag the topic all over the place. Salespeople will have a tough time knowing where they are in the sales process and whether or not they have imparted important product information. They may never get an opportunity to summarize and properly ask for the order. In short, they've lost control. The whole idea behind proper and effective selling skills training is to give salespeople the tools they need to control and to direct the sale—saving their time and the time of their potential clients and accomplishing more of what they intend to do.

It's okay if your buyer is most interested in the presentation part of the sales process—if he considers it to be the main show. It should feel that way to him. It's a show you've designed and built just for him based on your preparation, the establishment of rapport, and your qualifying and discovery questions. Your job is to present *the right solution*, not a one-size-fits-all solution. Your custom solution will persuade your buyer that your product is the right answer for his particular wants, needs, and desires. It will provide your buyer with the information he needs to make wise buying decisions.

Effective presentation skills increase the probability of your buyer taking immediate action. That's because a clear presentation leads to understanding, but it's far from being the main show.

THE MAIN SHOW

If the presentation is the center of attention for the buyers, the main show for the salesperson is the close. Here's what you do during the close:

1. summarize their challenge,
2. review the benefits your solution provides, and
3. ask the buyer to take immediate action in order to own your offering.

Note: During this process, there may be some negotiation as to terms, type of investment, delivery date, and location.

The close is the main show, because the close is a time of decision. **Salespeople are paid to persuade buyers to take action.**

The presentation provided the information in a persuasive manner that led the buyer to the point of decision. The close includes those uncomfortable moments of uncertainty when the buyer balances precariously between action and inaction. Part of your service to the buyer is to guide her through those emotional and mental aspects of decision making, leading her to a conclusion that makes sense for her and for your company.

Most of the anxiety salespeople have during the sales appointment revolves around this step of the sales process. It's when you are most likely to hear the word *no*. The closing step in the sales process is covered in great depth in chapter 10.

WHEN "NO" REALLY MEANS "NO SALE"

On those occasions when the *no* you hear is truly a final one, the truth is, you still have a sale to make. This new sale is to win the opportunity to stay in touch with these folks. You may need to say something like this: "Sue, since you need to get some other things taken care of before taking advantage of the benefits of my product, I'd suggest we arrange a date and time to reconnect. You were talking about a two-month time frame. So what would be best for you—to meet again on a Wednesday evening at 7 p.m., like we did tonight? Or would you prefer to meet on a Thursday evening, which was our other option for this week?" Your goal, once again, is to keep the opportunity for the sale moving forward. Getting a commitment to revisit a potential client whose *no* means *not now* does just that.

Even in situations where a potential buyer is not going ahead but has stated that he likes your product, you can still ask for referrals. Just because he isn't in a position to purchase your product doesn't mean he doesn't know someone else who is. If he really does like what you're selling, he'll be open to suggesting it to others who might have a similar need and be more likely to make a purchase now. How to go about getting those types of referrals is the topic of chapter 18.

YOUR ATTITUDE ABOUT REAL *NO*S

Since self-motivation is the only real motivation there is, you have to decide how you're going to handle those real *no*s mentally and emotionally. Some trainers will tell you to never end the day on a "*no* sale"—to always make at least one more call after a "*no* sale." You have to decide what will work for you. It's important to find a way to reenergize yourself before tackling the next sales opportunity.

This is all part of your preplanning for presentations. Decide in advance how you'll react if you don't get the sale. In other words, don't let it be a shock to your system.

Remember, there are only three basic answers that potential clients will give you: "Yes," "No," or "Maybe."

Prepare as much as you possibly can, but also know that there may be factors you're not aware of in advance that could negatively impact the sale. If you don't build a system for yourself to handle failure and rejection in sales, you'll quit before you can make enough presentations to enjoy the lifestyle of the top selling pros.

One formula for handling the word *no* is to relate it to a *yes* or a closed sale. Using your own closing ratio, figure out how many contacts it takes you on average to make one sale. Then, consider how much you personally earn on average per sale.

For example, if you close one out of every five contacts, that means with those five contacts you would hear one *yes* and four *no*s. If you earn $1,000 per sale, each of those four *no*s you need to face gets you one step closer to that $1,000. Therefore, you can think of each "*no* sale" as having a value of $250.

The formula looks like this:

1 Closed Sale = $1,000
5 Qualified Contacts = 1 Closed Sale

1 *Yes* and 4 *No*s

Thus, each *No* = $250

This strategy assumes that your intentions and actions during each contact are to get a *yes*. You know that you will not get a *yes* at *every* sales appointment, but you also recognize that you *could* get a sale at any sales appointment. Based on that assumption, this strategy helps you maintain your focus on your activity level.

Get those four *no*s, and you'll be reaching for that $1,000 *yes* next. When you hear a definite *no*, you can then mentally say, *Thanks for the $250*, or whatever your particular dollar amount is. You then move on to your next sales opportunity feeling confident about being closer to a closed sale. This is a little mental game that will add more fun—and comfort—to your selling days.

SELLING AS A GAME

Think of selling as a game. It's a game based on strategy, training, and skill, just like any other game. Perhaps you are a sports fan. You enjoy the excitement and thrill of watching your favorite team as the game unfolds. How your favorite players respond to the unknown conditions and actions of the opposing team creates the entertainment that sports fans all over the world enjoy. It's parallel to the sport of selling.

Consider the notion that human persuasion is the ultimate sport. Each buyer is different. Each has:

1. a different starting point,
2. a different personality,
3. a different amount of money, and
4. different timing.

Yet in every sales appointment, common principles of persuasion apply. That means there is enough variety yet familiarity in each sales appointment to make every sales call an adventure in persuasion.

Your expertise about your product, your company, and your industry allows you to be of service to others. Part of the service you offer is helping your buyers explore all the options available to meet their needs, both before and after they say *no*. That is a service to be proud of and to be excited about.

The next chapter covers the various models for the sales process and introduces a foundational strategy for keeping the sale moving forward after buyers say *no*.

CHAPTER 2 KEY POINTS

- In selling, a *maybe* is to be treated like a *no* until it can be turned into a definite *yes*.
- A confused mind will always say *no*.
- It's better to give too little information and have buyers ask for more than to give too much information and lose buyers from information overload or boredom.
- If buyers consistently ask for more information after your initial closing attempt, then it is time to make an adjustment in your presentation.
- The buyer's *no* might mean "No, not right now."
- You always have to demonstrate your own level of competence as well as your product's benefits.
- In selling, the person asking the questions controls and leads the sale.
- Salespeople are paid to persuade buyers to take action.
- Even in situations where a potential buyer is not going ahead but has stated that he likes your product, you can still ask for referrals.

3. Lost in the Sale

The biggest pitfall most salespeople face is becoming lost in the sale. They follow the sales presentation or process they've memorized and have rehearsed very well. The sales presentation is finished. The potential client's questions and concerns have been addressed.

But then, the crucial part is upon the salesperson. It's time to actually close the sale. And unfortunately, sometimes the salesperson may not be confident about how to make a smooth transition to asking for the business. Average salespeople resort to dialogue that generates one-word answers rather than drawing out buyers to ensure they're ready to make a decision. Their dialogue might sound like this:

Salesperson: *"Do you have any other questions?"*
Buyer: *"Nope."*
Salesperson: *"Does what we discussed today make sense to you?"*
Buyer: *"Yes."*

Typical buyers do not say, "Jim, I think this is a great solution for my company. Let's do the paperwork so I can give you my purchase order number and get the delivery scheduled." They wait for the salesperson to orchestrate what happens next.

After all, thus far in the meeting, the salesperson has been in charge—asking questions, demonstrating the product, and responding to concerns. The fact that it's time to make a buying decision may not even occur to the buyer to be the next natural step in the sales process. He is waiting for direction. And average salespeople may not be sure how to direct that next step without the risk of turning off buyers. The result can be an awkward situation during which the buyer's feelings of confidence in the salesperson and the product can wither and die.

Does this scenario sound familiar? This is called being *lost in the sale*. It occurs when salespeople have adopted and followed a linear model of persuasion.

THE LINEAR MODEL OF PERSUASION

The linear model of persuasion looks like this:

Build Rapport → Present Solutions → Answer Questions

Many salespeople show up at meetings with potential clients, initiate some small talk, make a presentation, and answer questions. Then they default to wait-and-see selling as to what buyers do next *rather* than continuing to control the selling situation with a smooth transition into closing the sale. This linear model of persuasion can be a one-way road to becoming lost in the sale.

Once lost, many salespeople assume that if they keep repeating the reasons to buy and keep repeating them fervently enough, the buyer will eventually say *yes*.

Their thinking is this: *Whenever buyers hesitate to take action, just keep selling, pushing, and prodding until they buy.* Not only is that *not* the way to sell professionally, it doesn't sound like a fun way to fill your working hours each week, does it?

Then why do so many salespeople follow this model of persuasion?

1. Because it's the only one they have ever been taught. They don't realize they have a choice in how to approach their persuasion efforts.

2. The linear model works...sometimes. If you see enough people, most any plan will work sometimes. But in the long run, using this linear model can be costly. It can leave a lot of sales on the table plus annoy some potential clients in the process.

The linear model of persuasion helps salespeople get through the first few steps in the sales process, but in truth, it's not complete. That linear model contains two particular flaws.

1. It does not give the salesperson a way to track where they are throughout the entire sales process.

2. It is insufficient for working with buyers who do not follow the script and say *yes* at the end of the presentation or after their questions have been answered.

Most salespeople know whether they are off to a good start or a cold start right at the beginning of the sales call. They can tell if the buyers are warming up to them and if a level of comfort is being established. Also, most salespeople can gauge how well they are doing *during* the sales presentation. They know if the buyer is engaged in the presentation. They can tell if the buyer understands and agrees with what is being presented. Even during the question-and-answer stage, most salespeople can tell if the buyer is receiving their answers in a positive manner.

The primary challenge with the linear model is not in building rapport, presenting solutions, and answering questions. The biggest challenge is what happens when the end of the linear road has finally been reached. What do average salespeople do when the buyer appears to understand the value proposition, her questions have been answered, and...she does nothing? Average salespeople simply wait for buyers to say, "I'll take it."

At this point in the sale, average salespeople will default to repeating the same information, the same reasons to buy, until either the buyer gives in and asks for the product or the salespeople run out of things to say, pack up their materials, and leave—*without a sale*. Remember this:

Telling isn't selling.

TOPIC JUMPING

Linear-thinking salespeople can feel lost in the sales process when they hear *no* from potential clients anywhere except at the end of their presentation. They are just not prepared to make adjustments on the fly. They are prepared only to move to the next logical step in their linear sales model. And that's a real challenge.

The challenge is that what's logical to the salesperson is rarely logical to the buyer. In fact, salespeople are often caught off guard when potential clients jump all around in the sales process. Those salespeople try to follow rather than lead, and they end up completely losing control of the sales process.

In sales, logic is used by the buyers to rationalize decisions, but only after an emotional involvement has occurred. This is what makes it so critical for sales professionals to expect and work with buyers' tendencies to wander by guiding and controlling the process with the right words and actions. Good sellers do it so smoothly that the buyers never truly realize they're being guided.

For example, a professional tour guide points out only the attractions in which tourists have expressed interest. If there's no avoiding certain attractions, the guide works to make them interesting.

FOUR STEPS TO PERSUASION

As a professional salesperson, you simply cannot wait to see what the potential clients will do next, and you cannot allow buyers to control the sales flow by bouncing the topic all over the place. When you do, you're actually giving them the power to decide what happens next. Chances are that you will not like the direction in which they will take the sales appointment.

Persuasion is a simple process. There are only four critical steps:

1. Establishing Rapport
2. Identifying Needs
3. Presenting Solutions
4. Closing Questions

Even though persuasion is simple, it is not always easy, because people are complex. There are endless variations of dynamics when persuading buyers to take action. Always bear in mind that buyers have different:

- starting points,
- personalities,
- questions,
- timing, and
- money constraints.

There are enough variations to keep the sales process interesting for the sales professional—and in truth, potentially overwhelming.

Have you ever wondered, *Do I need to learn all the possible sales techniques before I can competently and confidently persuade my buyers to take action?*

The answer is no! **If you understand and perform the four basic activities of persuasion, you will enjoy a decent career in sales.** Will additional sales knowledge help you more effectively perform those four basic activities and increase your sales? Yes... but only once you have organized those strategies in a manner that helps you *use* them to your best advantage during sales appointments. A circular model of persuasion is being introduced in this book that allows sales professionals to organize all the teachings in the sales education universe in one easy-to-remember format so they can more easily apply them to closing more sales.

Proper selling involves asking the right types of questions. It's a simple process, but one that must be learned and followed. The dynamics for success between you and Mrs. X might be so different from the dynamics between you and Mrs. Y that an untrained observer may not recognize them as being the same sales process until you reach the end—two closed sales transactions.

Depending on how you received Mrs. X's contact information, your starting point in the sales process may be at an earlier step or a later step than that for Mrs. Y. They have different personalities, interests, desires, needs, money issues, and questions. The thought processes required to sell each the very same product may be extremely divergent.

To the uninitiated, this may seem overwhelming. The great news is that simple principles drive the sales process, regardless of the diverse and unique circumstances that accompany each sales scenario.

In short, when you understand the basic drivers of selling scenarios, you will be able to determine where your buyers are in the persuasion process and what activity you should perform next.

By the end of this book, you will understand the structure of a circular sales model from start to finish. That knowledge will enable you to sell *any* type of product or service in an efficient and effective manner. That expertise will allow you to have more fun, close more sales, and ultimately make more money.

CHAPTER 3 KEY POINTS

- The biggest challenge most sales professionals face is becoming lost in the sale.
- The fact that it's time to make a buying decision may not even occur to the buyer.
- The linear model of selling is usually insufficient for working with buyers who do not say *yes* at the end of the presentation or after their questions have been answered.
- Telling isn't selling.
- Logic is used by the buyers to rationalize decisions, but only after emotional involvement has occurred.

SECTION 2

—

The Circle of Persuasion

4. The Circle of Persuasion

To simplify the selling process, we want you to start following a road map of sorts that will help you to get and stay on course to the desired conclusion in a selling scenario—a closed sale. It's called the Circle of Persuasion. Here is what it looks like:

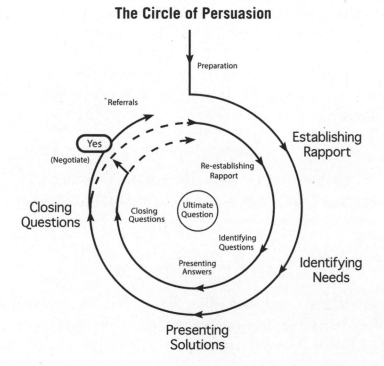

The Circle of Persuasion

Preparation

Referrals

Yes

(Negotiate)

Re-establishing
Rapport

Establishing
Rapport

Closing
Questions

Closing
Questions

Ultimate
Question

Identifying
Questions

Presenting
Answers

Identifying
Needs

Presenting
Solutions

Take a moment to go through the Circle. Look at each step. Do your best to keep this selling cycle in mind, as this will become the main focus of the book and, in effect, of your development of a unique and effective sales approach.

By studying this illustration, you will master the four basic activities of persuasion that will bring forth the biggest difference in your level of success in your selling career. The four key steps in almost every sales scenario are:

1. Establishing Rapport
2. Identifying Needs
3. Presenting Solutions
4. Closing Questions

Most important, this persuasion compass will help you to re-engage buyers when their response to step four is *no*.

Depending on where you are in the sales process, you have three potential options for what to do next. You will:

A. ask a question to gather information or clarify a point,
B. make a statement that provides answers to buyers' questions, or
C. remain silent.

There you have it. Four steps. Three potential actions. They are easy to understand and easy to remember. Here's a quick overview of the Circle of Persuasion:

ESTABLISHING RAPPORT

This is where you initiate small talk to break down any of those awkward barriers of resistance that are so common in selling situations. You will also demonstrate credibility during this phase in order to get buyers to relax with you and open up about their needs and expectations in the following step.

IDENTIFYING NEEDS

This is where you ask the right types of questions to assist you in determining whether or not you can actually help each potential client. The types and progression of questions you should ask— from establishing rapport to beginning the presentation—are covered in following chapters. Finally, you will learn a special set of questions that allow you to discover the true buying dynamics of each buyer. These questions will help you shape the emphasis of your presentation and close the sale during the initial sales call.

PRESENTING SOLUTIONS

The presentation is where you give buyers a solid reason to own your product or service. In reviewing features and benefits, you will learn how to sell the deeper value of your offering. You will learn how to sell your product's value against your cheaper competitors.

Many sales professionals think that the presentation is the main show. This belief stems from the false assumption that if you simply educate a person, she will buy. Not so. In the Circle of Persuasion you will learn that the presentation is only part of the introduction. The main show begins with the next stop around the Circle of Persuasion: closing questions.

CLOSING QUESTIONS

The closing of the sale—which begins when you ask the buyer to take action—is, in fact, the main show. All of your interaction with your buyer up to this point merely introduces the moment of decision. *Remember*: You are not paid to give presentations. You are paid to close sales.

You will learn the two most frequent mistakes salespeople make at the end of their presentations—and the important distinction between trial closing and direct closing.

THE INNER CIRCLE

Congratulations! You completed the outer circle of the persuasion model and have led your buyers to the first moment of decision. One of three results will occur.

1. The buyer wants to own.
2. The buyer wants to negotiate.
3. The buyer presents a question or concern.

At this point, the Circle of Persuasion can really provide a valuable insight. When answering a question or addressing a concern, you perform the same four steps that you followed to lead the buyer to the first decision point! The second time around, each step happens more quickly and will bring you even closer to a closed transaction.

1. Re-establishing Rapport

The first step in responding to a question or concern is to re-establish rapport. Always remember that for many buyers, making any kind of major decision is uncomfortable. Re-establishing rapport, like the other steps in the inner circle that will follow, takes just a fraction of the time to accomplish, but it's critically important. You may say, "I'm glad you asked that," or "Thank you for bringing that up." In just one sentence, you communicate that it is all right that your buyer didn't say *yes* right away. Your goal is to relax the buyer so you can prevent her wall of sales resistance from gaining strength.

2. Identifying Questions

You do not have to respond immediately to a question or concern! You can choose to ask additional questions that clarify the buyer's concerns. You may ask, "Is this your only question?" Or, "After we address your questions, will you be ready to take action today?" The more you understand the context of their questions and concerns, the more effectively you can respond and move them to take action.

3. Presenting Answers

Now that you understand the context of their question, you are ready to answer. Your answer is in itself a brief presentation. It is just a fraction of the length of your earlier, full-blown presentation. At the end of your mini presentation, it is critically important to ask...

4. Closing Questions

After responding to questions and concerns, ask your buyers again to take action. The person who asks the questions controls the direction of the sales appointment. When your buyers ask questions, answer them clearly, and *then complete your answer with a question of your own that asks them to take immediate action.*

THE ULTIMATE QUESTION

Where does the process of persuasion end? Do you keep going around in circles? No. At some point, you will decide that you have answered all of your buyer's questions and that he is now simply procrastinating.

Your final step is to effectively ask your buyer to take immediate action. If you made the effort to make a thorough presentation, don't end the sales appointment until you ask the ultimate question! You have nothing to lose and everything to gain.

During the final steps around the Circle of Persuasion you will need to employ negotiation skills with some buyers. Sometimes buyers want to change the terms of the sale. You will need to know how to distinguish *negotiation requests* from *concerns* and the four steps of preparing for a negotiation. Negotiation involves all your selling skills; it truly is the ultimate demonstration of your ability to persuade. *Bear in mind*: When a buyer starts to negotiate with you, that means he has decided he wants your product. It's now just a matter of working out the details.

TAKING A STEP BACK

There are subtle nuances and steps within each aspect of the Circle of Persuasion that could create the "say no" thought process in the buyer. Before delving into the details of the Circle of Persuasion, it's important to understand what could happen early on in the sales process to cause the buyer to question or fear the possibility of owning your product. That's the subject of chapter 5.

CHAPTER 4 KEY POINTS

- Four steps to memorize: (1) Establishing Rapport, (2) Identifying Needs, (3) Presenting Solutions, and (4) Closing Questions.
- Three potential actions: (1) ask a question, (2) make a statement, and (3) remain silent.
- The presentation is where you give the buyer real reasons to own your product or service.

- Always remember: You are not paid to give presentations. You are paid to close sales.
- The first step in responding to a question or concern is to re-establish rapport with the buyer.
- You do not have to respond immediately to a question! You can choose to ask questions that clarify the buyer's concerns.
- Your final step is to ask your buyer to take immediate action.

5. Did the Buyer's No Start with You?

Let's back up for a moment and start at the very beginning. Not with the beginning of the sales appointment. Not even with the first contact you had with the buyer. Long before the sales process began, there was you and your belief about what you do for a living. Let's have a heart-to-heart discussion about you and your thinking as it relates to your selling career.

It is difficult, if not impossible, for you to give your best efforts to selling, to be your best you, if you do not believe in what you are doing. This is true in most areas of life. It is especially true in selling. **If you don't believe in what you're selling, no one else will, either.**

ARE YOU SELLING FROM AN EMPTY WAGON?

The sales profession demands your very best at all times. It is not like working at a manual task where regardless of whether you are tired, angry, hungry, or distracted in your thoughts, you can still accomplish your task at an acceptable level.

Selling is different because if you're not at your best, it will show immediately in the results you're getting. Selling skills, when used well, are practically invisible to your buyers. When you're at your best in selling, buyers just think you're a very likable person who happens to have great knowledge about your product.

But when you're not at your best, selling strategies are far from invisible. In fact, when you have poor skills or a poor attitude, it will practically exude from your pores. It will be blatantly obvious that you're attempting to use learned strategies and tactics on your buyers. It's difficult to hide how you feel about your profession or your product from your buyers. They can immediately sense if you do not like your company, your product, or your industry. They can sense if you do not want to be working with them or if you do not personally like them.

Who you are, what you believe, and how you manage your feelings affect how much you accomplish in selling and how well you do your job. So let's examine some of the complex thoughts and feelings that each of us experience as humans and see how they directly relate to sales performance.

ARE YOU TRULY CONVICTED?

What's your current level of conviction about your industry and your specific products? There's a maxim in the sales industry: "You can't sell from an empty wagon." What does that saying mean to you?

The idea it conveys is that if you want to excel in the sales profession, you must have something of value to sell. While potential clients must perceive that value before they will buy, it is even more important that you, the sales professional, perceive it first.

Do you think it is possible that some salespeople sell products or services they don't believe in? The truth is that many salespeople are not fully convinced:

1. of the value of their products or services,
2. of their pricing structure,
3. that their company provides quality customer service or has the best interests of their clients in mind, or
4. that their sales manager or company management is competent.

What do you believe about your company and your industry? This is a time for some serious thought. Your level of conviction about what you offer to clients and potential clients directly affects your compensation. In fact, your compensation is a mirror reflection of the amount of service you give. Most people find it difficult to provide good service if they don't believe in what their products do for their clients. Your level of conviction also directly affects your job satisfaction. It directly affects your internal access to your sales potential. If you don't feel great about what you do, you will subconsciously limit your ability to truly excel in your endeavors.

Lots of salespeople are so hungry to learn the next technique to increase their sales revenues that they basically skip right over the internal dynamics that are so vital to how well they use any of those skills. How you feel about this topic—your internal level of conviction about the sales profession and the product you represent—is the foundation for long-lasting and consistent performance throughout your entire career. Taking a few moments to examine your beliefs will pay handsomely in increased sales revenues.

First and foremost, think about your answers to these questions:

- Why are you selling these particular products and services?
- What excites you about them?

Some might think we are asking about the features and benefits of what you sell. Actually, we are talking about a deeper set of reasons—why *you* are involved in your industry and with your company. Does it excite you to see new buyers make their lives easier or more profitable because of what you offer them? Take a moment to make a list of the value your buyers receive from:

- your industry,
- your company,

- your products and services, and
- your personal expertise and service.

Now that you have written down the exciting aspects of your sales environment, write down the areas in which you may be harboring shadows of doubt or concern.

- Is it your pricing structure?
- Is it the quality of your product?
- Is it the level of your company's customer service?
- Is it the financial stability of your company?
- Is it bad press about your industry or your company?

Get it out in the open. Putting down on paper what is bugging you about a situation can help release the hidden emotional pressure that subtly undermines your sales efforts. Making a list allows you to more objectively look at your concerns. It allows you to compare those fears and shadows of doubt to all the exciting aspects of your sales environment that you love... and it can create a perspective that minimizes negative feelings.

This process will give you more access to your internal resources to help you excel in your career. So make a list of the not-so-exciting aspects of your sales environment. Then consider how you might be letting them hold you back. Decide what you can do to change that level of impact. Then act upon what you can change. And, to paraphrase the Serenity Prayer, accept the things you cannot change.

If you conclude that the product you sell isn't a very good one, it's time to find something better to sell. Too many salespeople make the mistake of looking for products that are easy to sell or that pay high "commissions" (which we refer to as "fees for service.") There is a certain logic in that thought process. However, a better way to seek out a product to sell is to find something that you believe in. The truth of the matter is that people don't buy with logic. They buy emotionally then defend their decisions with logic. Salespeople must be *sold* on what they sell. They must choose a product they can emotionally connect with, then apply their logic to rationalize the buying decision.

A quick dose of reality: if you are looking for a perfect company or a perfect product, it's going to be a long search. No company or product is perfect. Companies are made up of people, and people aren't perfect. If you think you have to find a perfect company before you can give your best efforts, then you will never reach your full potential.

The great companies of the world are not perfect companies. The great companies of the world provide good value and good customer service, and they are quick to respond when they drop the ball. That is a lot different from being a perfect company.

So the question is not whether your company or your product has some imperfections. The question is whether your company provides enough real value to its clients for you to sell with true conviction.

CHAPTER 5 KEY POINTS

- It's difficult to hide how you feel about your profession or your product from your buyers.
- If you don't believe in what you're selling, no one else will, either.
- Your level of commitment about what you offer to clients and potential clients directly affects your compensation.
- The greater your sales skills, the more choices you will have about where you can work and how much compensation you will earn.

6. Did You Establish and Maintain Sufficient Rapport?

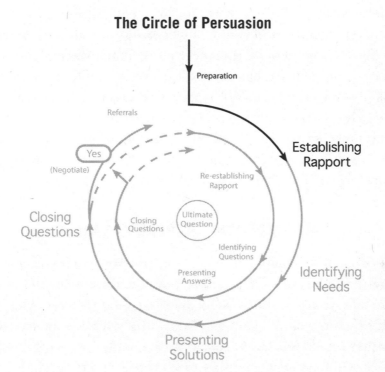

The Circle of Persuasion

Preparation

Referrals

Yes

(Negotiate)

Re-establishing Rapport

Closing Questions

Closing Questions

Ultimate Question

Establishing Rapport

Identifying Questions

Presenting Answers

Identifying Needs

Presenting Solutions

Never forget that the first step in the sales process, when you are meeting with potential clients, is to establish rapport with them. This is a common courtesy—an accepted norm. It allows you the opportunity to establish yourself as someone who is likable and on their side—an expert they can really trust.

It's critical to any selling situation to establish rapport before getting down to business.

If you fail to complete this step or skip it altogether, you will increase your chances of hearing the word *no* later in the sales process. It's a rare occasion when you can jump right into qualifying a potential client, then present your offer—although in some types of selling, it's possible to make sales without working too much on this step.

An example of this might be providing emergency services such as heating repair. Buyers will want to assume that you are a competent representative of your company who can handle their needs quickly. They may not care about whether or not you and they have much in common. In their minds, the commonality is simply that you're both working to resolve the same urgent dilemma. All you need to do is to be kind and professional as you go about your job.

But these situations are rare. In nearly all other selling situations, establishing a real rapport is crucial to establishing your competence and credibility with buyers.

WHY RAPPORT INCREASES SALES

In most selling situations, the level of rapport you establish will directly affect your ability to close the sale. Buyers are more likely to answer your questions about their needs if they feel you have their best interests at heart. **Well-established rapport creates a comfort level that leads to trust.** When rapport is established, people will pay more attention to your presentation. They'll also give more credence to what you say as you handle their questions and concerns.

So let's take it from the beginning of the sales appointment and see what you're doing right and how you might improve in building rapport.

You have arrived at the buyer's place of business, or your buyer has entered your place of business. You are now face-to-face with the buyer. How do you begin your sales process?

1. **Smile.** This may seem trite, but you would be surprised at how few people have natural smiles on their faces as they go about their days. Play a game by catching your reflection in mirrors or windows throughout a single day, and count how many times a smile is there. It doesn't count if you smile after your eyes make contact with your reflection. If you're not outwardly happy to meet with these potential clients, you're starting the process from a deficit standpoint.

This same strategy applies for telephone sales. Your smile can be "heard" in the tone of your voice. Consider keeping a small mirror on your desk where you can glance at your face several times throughout the day. Count how many times you catch yourself smiling or not. If the numbers weigh heavily on the "not smiling" side of things, then write the word *SMILE* in capital letters and tape it to the bottom edge of your computer screen or somewhere else where you'll see it frequently throughout your day. Then, smile before you take or make any call. It may sound silly, but trust us, it's important.

2. **Make small talk.** Your goal is to discover subjects that are of interest to your buyers and to enjoy a few minutes of informal chitchat. These topics may include family, sports, pets, hobbies, travel, cars, and so on.

Note: Unless there's something unusual going on, try to avoid the topic of the weather. It's just too trite, and of course, no one knows how to change the weather. The conversation will go nowhere.

Why do we encourage you to invest valuable time discussing non-business topics? It's because selling situations tend to generate a certain amount of skepticism or even fear in the minds and hearts of buyers. This is a learned reaction by your buyers, and it's what provides the building materials for those walls of sales resistance. Unfortunately, there are lots of perceptions about sales reps, and most of them are bad. Your potential clients have been told over the years:

- about bad experiences where someone made a mistake when spending their money, or
- that salespeople are crooks and are not to be trusted.

Just look at how the movies and television portray salespeople and you will understand. Building rapport helps you break down some of those fear barriers that most people have learned.

But there's more than that. Strong salespeople like to invest a few moments in letting buyers know that they see them as more than just...well, buyers. For other salespeople, it allows them the opportunity to relax and to become more comfortable before getting down to business. After a full day of tasks, traffic, and time pressures, it's nice to take a deep breath and to slow down for a couple of minutes before delving into another sales process.

Small talk is one of two primary ways to establish rapport. The second way to establish rapport is through our nonverbal behavior—that will be covered later in this chapter. But for now, remember these insights:

- Rapport is the oil that runs the engine of persuasion.
- Rapport buys you time to make your presentation and address concerns.
- Rapport increases the probability that buyers want to do business with you.

- Rapport grants you more forgiveness if you don't express yourself clearly or if you make a mistake.

THE THREE PRINCIPLES OF RAPPORT

There are three principles of rapport. They will help you understand why establishing and deepening rapport will increase the probability that your potential clients will buy from you:

1. Buyers like salespeople who are like them

Have you noticed how friends adopt each other's behaviors? Friends tend to talk to each other at a similar speed and with a similar volume. Friends tend to adopt similar behaviors such as their postures, facial expressions, and gestures. This same exchange of behaviors occurs when you establish rapport with buyers. You and your buyers will gradually begin to adopt similar behaviors. As your behavior becomes more like theirs, you make it easier for your buyers to like you.

If you doubt this, think about the last time you were with someone who used drastically different postures and gestures than you do. At first, you would have been uncomfortable—trying to recognize what those postures and gestures meant. In effect, you were trying to translate his body language into something to which you could relate. Once the understanding was there, you probably felt more comfortable around him. It wasn't a matter of whether or not the other person was likable. It was more along the lines of whether or not you understood him.

Jon Berghoff has a wonderful quote in Susan Cain's bestselling book *Quiet*: "People don't buy from me because they understand what I'm selling. They buy because they feel understood." That's the goal of establishing rapport—to help your potential clients feel that you understand them. When done properly, that under-standing will lead to a level of like and trust.

What does being likable have to do with closing more sales? The significance is explained in the next two principles:

2. Buyers tend to trust likable salespeople

It's human nature, and it's true most of the time. It is especially noticeable with people you hardly know. Buyers who like you will trust what you say about your product to a greater degree than buyers who don't like you. And working against this reality of human behavior will adversely affect your persuasiveness with your buyers. You become likable when you do and say things that put others at ease.

3. Buyers like to buy from likable salespeople

Have you ever had a sales rep you did not like try to sell you some-thing? Perhaps you didn't like this salesperson's personality or how he spoke. Did you want to do business with this salesperson? Probably not. Unless driven by an immediate necessity for the product, most buyers do not want to do business with salespeople they don't care for.

Please note that rapport is a *penalty* situation rather than a *reward* situation. What that means is just because buyers like you does not automatically mean they will reward you with a pur-chase. However, if they do not like you, they will probably not do business with you. The penalty for lack of rapport is losing the sale early on in the sales appointment.

As an example, a salesperson can work for an industry-leading, reputable company, but if buyers perceive that salesperson as arrogant and condescending, they will be less willing to make a purchase. Their decision is not because of the value or pricing of that leading company's products and services, but because the salesperson was simply not seen as likable.

That is the reality of persuasion. You must establish and maintain rapport during your entire sales appointment.

HOW TO INCREASE YOUR RAPPORT WITH BUYERS

Building rapport with other people is a skill that can be learned, just like learning to drive a car. There are very specific elements to this skill, rules that apply, and various strategies for implementing those elements and rules.

There are two basic methods for establishing rapport:

1. verbally—through the meaning of the words you speak
2. nonverbally—with your behavior

Let's go deep into each topic:

1. Verbal rapport

The method most frequently used by salespeople to establish rapport with their buyers is to talk about subjects of common interest. For example, as you enter the client's office, take a moment to glance around the room.

- If you see a stuffed bass hanging on the wall of your buyer's office, you would ask questions about fishing.
- If you see family pictures on your buyer's desk, you would ask questions about family.
- If you see sports trophies, miniature cars, or pictures of foreign travels, you would ask questions about those topics.

- If you're working on a business-to-business sale, you might ask questions about the company and how long your buyer has been with them.

Small talk is a great way to verbally establish rapport. And as noted, a quick glance around the buyer's office as you come in will tip you off as to where her real passions lie. The real challenge occurs, of course, when the buyer isn't talkative and there aren't any clues in the office.

Salesperson: *"Do you have any kids?"*
Buyer: *"Nope."*
Salesperson: *"Got any exciting trips coming up?"*
Buyer: *"Don't really like to travel."*
Salesperson: *"Do you have a favorite team that you follow?"*
Buyer: *"Not a sports fan."*
Salesperson: *"What do you do for fun? Do you have any hobbies?"*
Buyer: *"Not really."*
Salesperson: *"Uh…"*

If small talk is your only strategy for establishing rapport, then nontalkative buyers will add a serious chill to the entire sales appointment, and this will diminish your probability of closing the sale. The good news is that these nontalkative buyers will also be nontalkative with the competition.

One verbal strategy that you might employ when you encounter a quiet buyer is to help the potential client realize that you are just like him in many ways. Here is a sample of what you might say: "You know, when I'm not working, I'm a consumer just like you. What I hope to find when considering any purchase is someone with excellent product knowledge who can answer most of my questions.

My job here today is to be someone you rely on for information. So please feel free to open up and share with me your questions and concerns regarding this product, and let's see how I can help you."

This kind of approach basically attempts to assure potential clients that you are on their side in this situation—that you are there to help them.

2. Nonverbal rapport

The second method for establishing rapport with buyers is through your nonverbal actions. How you use your voice and your physiology during the sales appointment will affect your level of rapport with your buyers. By *voice* we mean the tone, volume, and speed at which you speak. *Physiology* refers to your posture, facial expressions, and gestures.

Be verbally and nonverbally consistent in your communication with buyers during sales appointments. If your words praise the value of your product, but your voice and body communicate a sense of uncertainty or hesitation, your persuasive ability will be diminished. To paraphrase a popular saying: your actions during a sales appointment will speak louder than your words.

If the *meaning* of your words with your potential clients continually conflicts with your *nonverbal communication*, it is time to reexamine your level of conviction about your company, its product or services, and your love for the selling profession.

As discussed in chapter 5, your level of conviction directly affects your persuasiveness and, subsequently, your sales results. Relevant to this chapter, your level of conviction is subtly communicated to buyers through your tonality and physiology. You have few secrets from your buyers!

Let's examine in detail how your tonality and physiology impact your sales appointments.

1. Tonality

Tonality refers to how you use your voice to speak during your sales appointment. If you primarily sell over the phone (with no video conferencing), your tonality is your *entire* nonverbal communication!

How you speak during your sales appointments will powerfully communicate your enthusiasm and conviction for your product. In contrast, wait-and-see salespeople believe that the value of content alone is what persuades buyers to take action. They think, *Sure, enthusiasm is helpful, but really, buyers either want to take action or they don't.* So the wait-and-see salespeople drone their way through the presentation, paying little attention to how the presentation is delivered. When buyers don't leap to purchase the product, the wait-and-see salespeople shrug and blame fate for not sending them more enthusiastic buyers.

Don't make that mistake! How you deliver the content of your presentation directly affects the persuasiveness of your presentation. How you ask your buyers to take action directly affects the probability of their taking action. The three most persuasive elements of tonality are:

a) Volume

Pay attention to the volume of your voice and the volume of the buyer's voice. It's important. Do you speak to every buyer at the same volume? No. Many salespeople believe that to speak with enthusiasm they must speak loudly. That is not necessarily true. You can speak quietly or loudly yet still communicate with enthusiasm.

How loudly should you speak with buyers? By applying the three principles of rapport to your tonality during your sales appointments, you will adjust the volume and intensity of your voice to that of your buyer.

Ideally, you will match the buyer's speed and volume of speech within the first ninety seconds of contact. When the buyer speaks loudly, you will want to increase the volume of your voice close to his. He could be speaking loudly because he is hard of hearing. He may just be a normally loud speaker.

Note: Be aware of your surroundings if you feel the need to speak more loudly than is normal for you. You do not want it to appear that you and the buyer have gotten into a shouting match.

When a buyer speaks quietly, decrease the volume of your voice. You do not need to match the volume of your buyer's voice exactly, but come relatively close. The idea is to make her as comfortable as possible with you. Close enough is usually good enough.

Consider the perspective of your buyer. If she is soft-spoken and you speak loudly to her, is it possible she might assume you are a typical blustery salesperson? You could, in effect, push her away.

On the other hand, if your buyer speaks with a booming, powerful voice and you speak in a mild, quiet manner, is it possible he might think that you lack confidence in your company, in its products, or in yourself? The answer is yes. He may then attempt to dominate the sales process, and you may lose control.

The issue is not whether speaking loudly or quietly is more persuasive. In each example, the challenge is created by the *difference* in volume between you and your buyer. Matching tonality is a penalty situation. Too much of a difference in volume will distract your buyer from the message of your presentation and will often lead to a no-sale situation. Make it a habit to talk to your buyer in a similar volume to what he uses, but within the natural range of your voice.

b) Speed

Again, this is important. Do you speak at the same speed during every sales appointment? Applying the principles of rapport, you should speak at a speed similar to that of your buyer. In misunderstanding the expression of enthusiasm, some salespeople believe that speaking enthusiastically equates to speaking faster. That is not true. You can speak either slowly or quickly with enthusiasm.

Frequently, speed and volume are lumped together in the minds of salespeople. The faster they speak, the louder they speak. Often, they are simply unaware of doing either. But your buyers may become very aware of your speed of speech if it differs from how they speak... and they can be turned off by it.

The issue is not the value of fast speaking versus slow speaking. The issue is the disruption of rapport caused by the contrast between your verbal behavior and the buyer's verbal behavior. This is the key to this entire concept—not to be drastically different in behavior or tone, but to find and work in the range that the buyer finds most comfortable.

If your buyer speaks deliberately and you speak much more quickly, what might be her impression of you? Is it possible she might assume you are a typical fast-talking, pushy salesperson? But if the buyer is a busy type-A personality who speaks quickly, what would he think about a slow-talking salesperson? Is it possible he might assume you are unmotivated or, worse, slow-witted? The takeaway of this topic is to speak at a similar rate of speed as your buyers.

c) Enunciation

A frequently overlooked area of tonality is speaking with clear enunciation. The principle to remember here is that a confused mind says *no*. **If your potential clients understand only 80 to 90 percent of what you say, their automatic response will be to say *no*.**

Enunciation is particularly important in the first few minutes of the sales appointment, when the buyer is getting used to your voice and your approach. During that brief window of time, your buyer will form an impression of you that may be difficult for you to change later in the sales process. If you are not speaking clearly, the buyer may decide you are not worth the effort of trying to understand. Wouldn't it be sad if you invested the time and energy to arrange a sales appointment only to lose the sale in the first few minutes because you didn't speak clearly?

Clearly enunciating your words is also critical when leaving voice mail messages. Imagine a busy potential client listening to ten or more voice mail messages. He listens to your voice mail and at the end hears you mumble or rush through your name or your callback number. Do you think the potential client will bother to replay your message several times to decipher your indistinct words? Probably not. Speak clearly enough to be understood, because when potential clients do not understand what you are asking, the easiest path of action for them is to do nothing.

2. Physiology

If you call on buyers in person or via video chat, be aware that the majority of the communication about your level of conviction and enthusiasm comes from your physiology. Actions really do speak louder than words! Below are several ways to create nonverbal actions that communicate the same message as the words of your presentation and close.

Note: Before *every* video call, start your camera and look carefully at what your potential clients will see.

- Is your desk a mess? If so, it will send the message not that you're busy but that you are simply disorganized.
- Is there a picture in the background that might be distracting?

- How about an open door where people are walking by?
- Could that plant behind you look like it's growing out of the top of your head?
- Is the lighting in the room dark or casting a ghoulish shadow?

We're not suggesting that you go to the lengths of staging your office for a broadcast-quality video production, but do what you can to keep anything but your alert posture and smiling face from grabbing the potential client's attention.

a) Posture

A powerful way to establish rapport with the buyer is to maintain a similar posture to theirs. Applying the principles of rapport, when the buyer sits up straight, you shift to a more upright posture. When the buyer sits back in a relaxed posture, then you relax your posture—but perhaps not as relaxed as your buyer's posture. Close enough is good enough.

Your objective is not to mimic your buyer's physiology. Rather, it is to avoid opposite behaviors. Most buyers will not consciously notice your posture, but they will notice if they feel comfortable with you. A contrast in postures may make a buyer feel uncomfortable. If the buyer is sitting upright at a desk full of work, and you sit back in your chair and assume a casual, relaxed posture, what might she think about you? That you are unmotivated? Even worse, that you do not respect how busy she is?

If the buyer sits back in a relaxed posture and you lean forward in an upright posture, what might he think about you? He may feel you are a pushy, aggressive salesperson anxious to get him to buy. In short, do your best to sit or stand in a posture similar to your buyer's.

There are two basic types of postures:

Symmetrical

A *symmetrical* posture means you squarely face the buyer. Sitting or standing, your shoulders and hips are equally distant from the buyer's. When sitting, your legs are not crossed and both feet are on the floor. When standing, you place equal weight on both legs, not leaning against the wall or turned to one side.

Asymmetrical

An *asymmetrical* posture means your shoulders and/or hips are pointed slightly to the side so the buyer looks across your body at an angle. Your head must be turned at a slight angle to face your buyer. Crossing your legs also creates an asymmetrical posture.

Which type of posture is most advantageous for your sales appointments? Initially, it may seem that symmetrical postures are more appropriate for business. You are there for business, not a social visit. Therefore, a formal posture is more appropriate. That was probably true in past decades. However, this could be unconsciously interpreted as an aggressive stance. Because the first objective in the sales appointment is to establish rapport, matching the posture of your buyer may include assuming a more relaxed, asymmetrical posture. It also allows you to demonstrate with your body language that you are on your buyer's side.

Symmetrical postures are more formal and communicate trustworthiness and authority. They show that you are focused on business. Asymmetrical postures are less formal and communicate that you are relaxed and at ease. So you will want to use both at the appropriate times.

Given the information above, now which type of posture would you say is most advantageous for your sales appointments? The answer depends on the posture of the buyers. *Remember the first principle of rapport: buyers like salespeople who are like them.* If buyers are in a relaxed, asymmetrical posture, then assume a similar asymmetrical posture, at least during the initial rapport-building phase of the sales appointment. After you have established rapport and are ready to shift the conversation toward business, you can smoothly shift your posture to something more formal. The key word here is *smoothly.* Any abrupt or sudden change in your posture may subconsciously trigger fear or resistance in your buyers.

This brings us to one of the most powerful advantages of establishing rapport with the buyer. As previously noted, people who are in rapport tend to trade behaviors. Because you nonverbally established rapport with the buyer early in the sales appointment, when you decide to assume a more attentive posture for your presentation, the buyer is more likely to follow your shift in posture. You can nonverbally transition your buyer into a more advantageous selling environment! **When the buyer follows your shift in posture, that is a solid and important indication that you have established sufficient rapport, and she is interested in hearing more of what you have to say.**

If the buyer does not follow your shift in posture, she has given a nonverbal cue that you have not yet fully engaged her level of interest. That may not be the feedback you desire, but it is valuable information to know before you begin a presentation. If that occurs, it may be advantageous to shift back once again to a posture similar to the buyer's and to ask more questions to confirm her openness to hearing your presentation.

Note: Occasionally, you may have sales appointments with visually attractive members of the opposite sex. It may be tempting to sit back and enjoy a relaxing few minutes as you chat with this person. This small talk may not necessarily be for the purpose of moving your sales appointment forward, but just for the sake of small talk with a visually attractive human being. Be forewarned: your buyer can always tell the difference.

From a business perspective, consider that these people probably hear the same trivial small talk from vendors, salespeople, and customers all day long. If you want to stand out from your competition and from all the other salespeople they encounter, be professional. Be pleasant, look them in the eye, and maintain an air of professionalism that nonverbally says that you are there strictly for business. If they choose to chat you up for a few minutes, fine. But remain alert for signals that they are ready to move forward in the sales presentation.

b) Proximity

Your rapport with buyers will be affected by how close you stand or sit near them. If you crowd buyers by standing or sitting closer than they are comfortable with, you will break the rapport you have established up to that point.

Americans typically prefer a comfort zone of twenty-four to thirty inches of space. How do you know if you are sitting or standing too close to buyers? The answer can be seen in their behavior. If buyers lean away or step back, you are probably too close.

Men, be especially aware of your proximity when talking to women. While some women may not mind if you get too close, other women will become so uncomfortable that you may actually lose the sale even before your presentation begins.

It's important here to also consider your body size in relation to your buyer's. If you are a large man selling to a petite woman or smaller man, you will not want to loom over the buyer. That may be perceived as threatening (consciously or not). In such cases, it's important to sit with your buyer as soon as possible to get you on a more level playing field, so to speak. If you're the small-statured one selling to people who are quite a bit larger than you, use a slightly more formal posture to command the attention that your body size does not.

Be aware that proximity is another penalty situation. Maintaining an appropriate proximity to the buyer is important. If you violate his comfort zone by standing or sitting too close to him, he will be more likely to say *no* to you. Make sure you do not crowd your buyer.

On a lighter note, proximity is something you can have a lot of fun with. The next time you are engaged in a standing conversation, take a step back and see if the others step or lean forward to follow you. If a potential client does, that is a good sign that you have engaged his interest!

c) Touching

As Shakespeare almost wrote, "To touch or not to touch, that is the question." That shameless paraphrase raises the important question of whether you should touch your buyers with a pat on their shoulder or back, touch them on the arm, give them a hug, or employ any other type of physical contact.

The advantage of appropriate touching is that a physical touch, when well received, warms the heart and increases rapport. The disadvantage is that an unappreciated touch can kill both rapport and the sale.

Some buyers are touchy-feely people. It is how they welcome people. Other buyers are less touchy or not at all feely. It is the not-at-all folks you need to be most aware of. Maybe you are one of them. If a salesperson touches a buyer against his wishes, the sales appointment is effectively over.

You never know what a touch means to a buyer. Men, this is especially true in your interactions with women. You simply don't know how your touch will be received. Given that lack of knowledge, do you want to risk losing the sale because of what you thought was a simple, inoffensive touch? The principle to remember is if in doubt, don't touch.

d) Handshake

Your handshake creates an impression about you as a sales professional. There is a range of firmness to employ in a handshake. It's important to pay attention so you use the right level for each client.

At one end of the spectrum is the crushing grip handshake. This is when too much pressure is applied to the buyer's hands. At the other end of the spectrum is the weak handshake, where too little pressure is applied. Neither handshake sets the tone for a pleasant sales call.

To properly shake hands, use a grip that closely matches the buyer's. *A one-size-fits-all handshake will not work for every buyer.* You must pay attention to each buyer's grip and adjust your own accordingly.

Handshaking is not an exact science. The objective is not to give the perfect handshake. Rather, it is to avoid giving a handshake that is noticeably different from your buyer's.

Will your handshake make or break the sale? Probably not, but consider that by the end of your sales call, the cumulative effect of a dozen of these "little things" can be a persuasive influence either in your favor or against you. Everything counts for something. Some actions count more than others, but everything counts for something.

Note to men: you may notice a unique style of greeting when introducing yourself to male blue collar workers. When shaking hands with many men, hesitation and timidity will not win you the level of respect that you desire. When you introduce yourself to a man, play him faceup. That means make eye contact, confidently reach out your hand for a shake, and boldly state your name. Give the man a firm handshake while maintaining eye contact. That favorable first impression will instantly establish rapport and positively enhance your persuasive opportunity with him.

e) Walking

The final area of physiology does not apply to all sales situations. If part of your sales appointment requires you to walk with a buyer to a different part of her office or job site, make sure you walk at the same pace. Motivated, busy buyers often walk at a fast pace. By walking as fast as the buyer, you nonverbally communicate that you are a motivated, busy salesperson, that you respect the buyer's hectic schedule, and that you're just like her.

If you do not keep up, the buyer may think you are unmotivated or lazy. Even if you do keep up but it appears that you have to rush to do so, you'll give the impression that you typically operate at a slower pace. Is that the impression you want to make?

Other buyers walk at a more deliberate pace. If you consistently step ahead of the buyer because your normal pace is faster, the buyer may think you are rushing him or are insensitive to any physical issue that may force him to walk slowly. Do not give your buyer a chance to wonder. Match the pace of your buyer and increase your level of rapport.

SELLING IN ACTION: TWO CASE STUDIES

To help you envision the strategies that have been covered thus far, two ongoing scenarios are provided in the ensuing chapters. In the first two instances, boldfaced questions are interspersed throughout the scenarios to help you recognize and choose how to apply the strategies to your selling situations. We will assume that you will understand the process and will do the same with the scenarios in chapters that follow.

Scenario 1: Business Sales Appointment

Kate parks her car and looks at the front of the potential client's small business. She thinks of three other appointments she has that day, all of which are with bigger potential accounts. She brushes that thought aside and reaches for her sales materials. Focusing on the present situation, she pulls out the brochures and forms that she will need for this meeting. She pops a breath mint in her mouth. Closing her eyes for several seconds, she visualizes the prospective client being friendly, responding favorably to her presentation, and approving the paperwork at the end.

Think about how you mentally and emotionally prepare for your sales calls.

Inside the office, Kate greets the receptionist pleasantly. The receptionist shows her into the office. Mr. Stevens is finishing a phone call and waves her over to his desk. Kate remains standing until he ends the call. He is tanned, possibly from working in the field or being on a beach. His hair is speckled with gray. Kate guesses he is in his early sixties.

CASE STUDY

"Sorry about that," Mr. Stevens apologizes as he sets the phone down. His deliberate pace of speaking and slight accent suggest Southern roots. "One of my teams in the field is having a challenging day. Here, please." He indicates for her to sit in a chair in front of his desk.

Kate extends her hand. "Kate Townsend." She looks him in the eyes and gives a firm handshake that matches the strength of his handshake. She hands him her business card before sitting down. As he reads her business card, she glances around the office. The wall behind his desk is filled with stuffed trophy game. The desk has autographed baseballs in small Plexiglas cases. Next to the baseballs are several pictures. One is of a young man posing next to two hunting dogs. The other pictures are of Mr. Stevens at professional sporting events standing next to a sports celebrity.

What do you notice when you enter a selling environment?

Mr. Stevens settles back in his chair. "Widget Corp," he states and then waits for her response.

Kate is sitting up in her chair with both of her feet on the floor, facing Mr. Stevens in a symmetrical posture. She does not see a wedding band on Mr. Stevens's finger or a picture of a woman on his desk. She draws no conclusions from that other than deciding to retain an air of formality to set the tone of their professional relationship. She smiles pleasantly but says nothing.

He continues. "Why would Widget Corp send one of their sales executives to call on a little ol' company like mine?"

Kate senses she is being measured. Smiling, she says, "Every client is important to us, sir."

"Please," he says quickly. "Call me Dean."

With the ice broken, she begins. "Thank you for your time in seeing me today, Dean. It was quite an adventure getting here."

"Yes, the streets are a bit tricky right now with all the construction. Did you have trouble finding us?"

"No real trouble. However, I'm thankful that I have GPS." She pauses as he chuckles and then continues, "How long has your office been at this location?"

What do you say to get the conversation started in a sales appointment?

"Almost fifteen years. When the airport expanded, we had to relocate. This is a bit off the beaten track, so we see very little walk-in traffic. But it's near the airport, and that makes it very convenient for shipping and travel."

Kate motions to the wall behind Mr. Stevens. "That's quite a widemouth bass you have there. It doesn't sing, does it?" she jokes, referring to a novelty item she occasionally sees in offices and homes.

Mr. Stevens laughs. "No, that's the real thing. Four pounds, six ounces. Caught it behind a cabin I have up north. Sounds like you know your fish. Do you like to fish?"

"I like to eat fish," Kate says without missing a beat. "My brothers went out fishing most every weekend when I was growing up. We lived near a large lake."

"Nothing like freshly caught, grilled fish," Mr. Stevens agrees.

Kate notices that he said, "a cabin I have," and not "a cabin we have," so she decides to avoid questions about a spouse unless he raises the subject.

What subjects are you careful to avoid during small talk?

Kate looks at the picture on his desk of the young man with the two hunting dogs. "The way he's dressed reminds me of my brothers. What was he hunting for?"

"Quails by day and raccoons at night." Mr. Stevens says with a chuckle. "That's my son, Dean Jr. Lots of good times hunting with those dogs."

Mr. Stevens doesn't offer any more information about family, so Kate moves on. She looks at the side wall with his diplomas. "University of Alabama. How did you end up starting a business all the way out here?"

Mr. Stevens scoffs. "Not by design. I can tell you that." Over the next few minutes, he describes going to work after graduation for a certain company, and how the problems at that company led him to start his own business.

Kate experiences conflicting emotions as she listens to Mr. Stevens tell his story. She is glad that he is engaged in conversation. That is the point of her questions. At the same time, she feels the pressing time constraints on her schedule. She has three other appointments that afternoon, calls and e-mails to return, and paperwork waiting at the office. Yet here she sits, spending precious minutes of the regular business hours making small talk with a potential client who is weaving a tale of his professional journey.

She takes a deep breath and relaxes her shoulders. The rapport she is building increases the probability of a sale and lays the foundation for client loyalty. Focusing her thoughts back on Mr. Stevens, Kate reflectively listens to encourage Mr. Stevens to continue sharing his professional story with appropriate words and phrases:

"Really?"

"What did you do next?"

"That's incredible."

Kate makes mental notes about certain challenges that Mr. Stevens faced in the past that could have been helped by using one of Widget Corp's products. At this point, Kate believes she has established a sufficient level of rapport, and she begins to narrow their conversation to business matters. Because Mr. Stevens trusts her enough to share his stories from the past, she believes he will open up and share his company's experiences with their current widget provider. Bridging his past business experiences to the present, she starts with a transition question: "So how did you get started using widgets?"

How do you determine when it is time to shift small talk to business talk?

Scenario 2: Residential Sales Appointment

Bob pulls his car in front of the sprawling ranch house in the wooded residential neighborhood. He turns off the engine and sighs. A quiet evening breeze blows through the open windows of his car as he listens to the birds chirping an evening song. So relaxing... He would rather be at home with his wife and two young children, but he is building his business to provide a great life for them. He joined Residential Widgets two years earlier. The big dreams he has for his family require a big income. He opens up his business folder and looks at a family picture of his wife and children on the beach. A smile crosses his face as he briefly relives the memories of that day.

How do pleasant emotions help you sell more effectively?

Bob checks the brochures he placed in the folder earlier that afternoon. Everything is set. He looks at the front door and visualizes the potential clients welcoming him into their home, engaging him in friendly conversation, asking questions during his presentation, and responding positively to his closing question. Snapping the folder shut, he gets out of the car and walks to the front door.

Mr. and Mrs. Johnson, both in their late fifties, greet him at the door. Bob shakes Mr. Johnson's hand firmly, matching his strong grip. Mrs. Johnson also extends her hand and gives him a mild handshake, which he responds to in-kind. They invite him into their living room. While still standing, Bob says, "Thank you so much for having me over this evening. Please call me Bob. Shall I refer to you as Mr. and Mrs. Johnson? What do you prefer?"

How do you determine what names to use when referring to your potential clients?

"Gary and Pat is fine," Mr. Johnson says in a booming deep voice.

Pat nods in agreement. Bob looks around the living room, noticing the family photographs and the artwork on the walls. With a smile, he asks, "So I can do a better job for you this evening, it would be best if we sat at the table. You don't mind, do you?" They agree, and he follows them into the kitchen, feeling glad that he has subtly established leadership early in the appointment.

As he and Gary sit down at the kitchen table, Pat offers to fix coffee. Bob doesn't want to have coffee breath as he sits in their vicinity. However, he likes to accept some form of hospitality when it is offered by potential clients. "No, thank you, but a glass of water would be great! Thank you."

How do you respond when potential clients offer you food or drink?

Gary sits back in his chair, so Bob assumes a similar posture. Bob notices the custom cabinets, granite countertops, and tiled kitchen floor. "What a beautiful kitchen!"

"Yes, we remodeled the entire kitchen three years ago," Pat says, beaming at her husband. "A twenty-fifth anniversary gift from Gary."

Bob adds, "I love the lighting under the cabinets."

Gary, who designed the kitchen with the remodeling contractor, is modestly enjoying the attention given to his kitchen design. "The LED technology gives Pat plenty of light without the heat. It's worked out really well."

As Pat places a glass of water on the kitchen table in front of Bob, he thanks her and continues. "I noticed your matching artwork when we were in the living room. Are those originals?"

Pat grins as she sits down next to Bob. "We are friends with a local artist. Doesn't she create beautiful work?"

Gary adds, "We have supported her artistic efforts for many years."

"They are wonderful," Bob replies with sincere appreciation. "What type of art talent runs in your family?" Bob words his question to include their family, because his next set of questions will be about their kids. Bringing their family into the conversation is the next step in directing their conversation toward business.

"We're not artists," says Pat, "but our daughter loves to make pottery." She points to several small pieces of decorative pottery standing on the corner of the counter. "Diane made those pieces over there."

"Those are fun. Is that her in the picture in the living room?" Bob asks, redirecting the conversation back to family.

"Yes," Pat replies. "That's her and our son, Scott. He moved to Seattle last year for a job with a technology company. Diane will finish college at the end of next year."

"An exciting time for your family," Bob affirms. He has now established a comfortable level of rapport. The conversation is pleasant and smoothly moves from topic to topic. Both potential clients are participating. Bob decides that their level of rapport is sufficient, and he proceeds to the next point around the Circle of Persuasion. He transitions to questions that identify Pat and Gary's needs.

"What will those changes mean for both of you when Diane eventually moves out of the house?"

How do you determine when it is time to shift from small talk about personal topics to discussing business-related topics?

CHAPTER 6 KEY POINTS

- It's critical to any selling situation to establish rapport before getting down to business.
- When rapport is established, buyers will pay more attention to your presentation.
- Unless there's something unusual going on, try to avoid the topic of the weather.
- Jon Berghoff: "People don't buy from me because they understand what I'm selling. They buy because they feel understood."
- Rapport must be established both verbally and nonverbally.
- If your words praise the value of your product, but your voice and body communicate uncertainty or hesitation, your persuasive ability may be diminished.
- Match your buyer's speed and volume of speech within the first ninety seconds of contact.
- Speak clearly. If your potential clients understand only 80 to 90 percent of what you say, their automatic response will be to say *no*.
- Understand and benefit from *symmetrical* and *asymmetrical* postures.
- When buyers follow your shift in posture, that is a solid and important indication that you have established sufficient rapport and they are interested in hearing what you will say next.

7. Identifying Needs

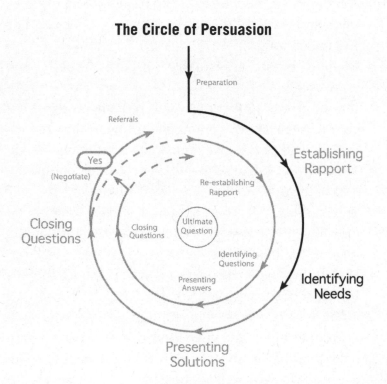

The Circle of Persuasion

Preparation

Referrals

Establishing
Rapport

Yes

(Negotiate)

Re-establishing
Rapport

Closing
Questions

Closing
Questions

Ultimate
Question

Identifying
Questions

Identifying
Needs

Presenting
Answers

Presenting
Solutions

You began the sales appointment by establishing a sense of rapport with the buyer through small talk and engaging in similar nonverbal behaviors. Now the time has come to begin steering the conversation toward the true business objectives of the sales appointment.

In order to get down to business, it's wise to develop and use a transition strategy as to what you say. Try something like this: "Mr. Kraft, let me begin by thanking you for the time we'll share here today. I hope we can consider this meeting somewhat exploratory—meaning my job as a [name of industry] professional is to show you how our dynamic company is helping businesses like yours."

By saying something like that, you are not only making the transition to business, but doing it in a way that doesn't add pressure to the situation. You're "exploring" what your company might do for them, not selling anything—yet.

Another strategy for transitioning from small talk to business talk is to simply introduce an agenda for your meeting. That introduction might sound something like this: "Robert, if you don't mind, let me explain how we'll proceed today. First, I'll share with you a little about our company so you will feel comfortable that we are the experts we profess to be. Then, I'll ask you some questions about your needs and hopes for finding the right solution. Next, if what we offer does provide a sound solution for your needs, we'll review that in as much depth as you would like. Our goal is that you feel truly comfortable with our solution before considering making any decisions. Also, please realize that neither my company nor I believe in high-pressure tactics. We realize our product is not right for everyone. It may or may not be right for you. I just hope you'll keep an open mind about it. Then, at the end of our time together, you tell me if you think our product is right for you. Does that sound okay?"

Now, some businesses, and some veteran salespeople, might cringe at the wording above, especially since you're voluntarily bringing up the idea that your product may not be right for them. However, this has been proven effective in hundreds of thousands of situations to reduce sales resistance. In essence, you've given buyers permission to say *no*. There's enough pressure in any sales situation that it's wise for you to relieve it as early as possible.

As you present your agenda or make your transition statement, sit up a little straighter. It's a nonverbal cue to buyers that it's time to pay attention. When they follow suit by sitting up or leaning in to listen to what you have to say, they're engaged. If they don't respond in that manner, you may have to shift gears and build a little more rapport.

Once you've made this transition, it's time to begin identifying the needs of the buyers by doing what top sales pros do best—asking questions.

QUESTIONS ARE THE ANSWER

Why is asking questions so important to a persuasive situation? Many salespeople think selling is all about making statements—*telling* buyers reasons to buy. Giving buyers the information they need to make a purchase is a vital part of the persuasion process. Remember: a confused mind says *no*. But what *you* say is never as persuasive as what buyers say to themselves. Whenever you ask a question, your buyers will mentally answer it, even if they don't say much out loud. Therefore, your questions should be designed to guide and to direct the answers buyers come up with about your product, your company, and your ability to serve their needs.

Buyers constantly ask themselves questions. Whether in their thoughts or spoken out loud, buyers ask questions such as:

- "Is this a good deal?"
- "What is the cost?"
- "Is this salesperson wasting my time?"
- "Can I buy this cheaper somewhere else?"
- "Will this company do what it promises?"
- "Does this salesperson really understand my situation?"

You cannot directly control how buyers will answer those questions. You can, however, influence the questions they ask themselves, which increases the probability of their coming up with the answers you want. That is the power of asking questions! When you help buyers ask themselves the right questions, the answers you want them to come up with are more likely to follow. In contrast, if you leave your buyers' questions to chance, you may not like their answers.

In summary, the person who asks the questions controls the conversation during a sales appointment. **However, if you ask questions but fail to show buyers that you are listening to their answers, your questions will do little to help you close the sale.**

To effectively identify the needs of buyers requires asking several layers of questions. It requires actively listening to determine the next question you must ask in order to encourage your buyer to continue talking. In this chapter, you will learn the types of questions and subsequent responses that encourage buyers to communicate key information necessary for them to take immediate action.

CLOSED-ENDED QUESTIONS

There are two basic types of questions you can ask buyers. The first type consists of closed-ended questions. These questions elicit one-word answers: a buyer answers either *yes* or *no*. Closed-ended questions have their place in the sales process, but when used at the wrong time they can put an abrupt end to a conversation instead of encouraging the buyer to tell you her wants and needs. Closed-ended questions to avoid when identifying needs begin with:

1. "Do you...?"
2. "Will you...?"
3. "Are you...?"
4. "Can you...?"
5. "Have you...?"

Here are some examples of questions with good content that are asked in an incorrect form. When used incorrectly, these questions discourage the buyer from revealing any information salespeople might find helpful in delivering relevant, compelling presentations:

Salesperson: *"Do you use our type of product very often?"*
Buyer: *"Yes."*
Salesperson: *"Will you be purchasing our type of product in the near future?"*
Buyer: *"No."*
Salesperson: *"Are you the person who authorizes new purchases?"*
Buyer: *"No."*

Because the closed-ended questions direct the buyer to give one-word answers, the salesperson doesn't learn *how* she uses the product, the reasons she won't be making a purchase in the near future, or *who* authorizes new purchases. When identifying the needs of your buyer, avoid asking closed-ended questions. They actively shut down the buyer's participation when you most want to hear from her.

OPEN-ENDED QUESTIONS

The second type of questions are open-ended ones. These are questions a buyer cannot answer with *yes* or *no*. These questions require real thought and elaboration on the buyer's part. When identifying needs, would you rather the buyer give short *yes/no* answers, or give full answers loaded with clues about why he wants and needs your products? (And yes, that was both an open-ended and a rhetorical question.)

There are basically six forms of open-ended questions. You are already familiar with them, though you may not have previously labeled these questions in this manner. The six open-ended questions start with the words:

1. "Who…?"
2. "What…?"
3. "When…?"
4. "Where…?"
5. "Why…?"
6. "How…?"

Open-ended questions require the buyer to provide valuable clues about his needs, desires, and buying procedures. Examples of open-ended questions are:

"What are the biggest challenges you face regarding your industry?"
"When is your busiest time of year?"
"What are your business objectives for this year?"
"How does your company make decisions about new purchases?
"What do you like and dislike about your current supplier?"

In short, the buyer can't answer your open-ended questions with a *yes/no* answer!

Consider how the types of questions you ask affect your sales appointments. Two salespeople ask buyers the same questions with one difference. The first salesperson asks open-ended questions. The second salesperson asks closed-ended questions.

After a full day of sales appointments, both salespeople return to the office and discuss their days.

• The first salesperson shares how each of his buyers talked nonstop about family, pets, sports, travel, or hobbies. Each time, the first salesperson asked for five minutes, and more often than not the buyer was still talking thirty minutes later.

• The second salesperson complains that the buyers hardly talked at all. Coincidentally, the second salesperson typically got very little time with the buyers. Often a buyer was so chilly during the presentation that the salesperson left with frostbite.

If you frequently experience buyers who provide little response to your questions, you may be asking too many closed-ended questions that elicit *yes* or *no* answers.

Remember that at this point in the sales appointment, participation alone is not enough. The rapport-building questions earlier in the sales appointment already elicited participation from the buyers. That objective was achieved. **The purpose of asking open-ended *business* questions after establishing rapport is to discover important information that's necessary to achieve a closed sale.**

LISTENING SKILLS

After you ask open-ended questions to encourage buyers to *begin* talking, you can encourage buyers to *continue* talking by implementing effective listening skills.

Have you ever spoken with people who are not paying attention to your conversation? Through their nonverbal behavior, you sense that their thoughts are elsewhere. Buyers will have a similar experience if they sense that the sales rep is not listening attentively. The salesperson asks a question...and halfway through the buyer's answer, the salesperson decides how to respond. The nonverbal transformation from listening to waiting occurs in an instant. Like a cat waiting to pounce upon its prey, the salesperson anticipates the moment when the buyer will stop talking. The salesperson may even make some interjections—such as

"Uh-huh. Yes, and— ...Okay. Right. Well...have you— ...hmm, sure"—hoping to regain control of the topic at hand.

Do you think your buyers can sense when you have stopped listening? (That was a closed-ended, rhetorical question.) Buyers may not be able to identify the specific nonverbal behaviors that indicate you have stopped listening, but they will know. When buyers know you are not listening to them, they may decide that answering your questions is a waste of time. That will not help you close the sale.

How can you show buyers you are actively listening? You can employ listening skills...just like you employed your questioning skills to get them talking. Let's review.

a. Nonverbal listening skills

In chapter 6, we discussed the importance of nonverbal communication to establish rapport. The same principles regarding your nonverbal behavior also apply to listening. When your buyer answers your questions, how do you nonverbally show her that you are listening? Possibilities include:

- maintaining eye contact
- nodding your head in agreement
- smiling or laughing at the buyer's humor
- facial expressions
- leaning forward slightly

While identifying your buyer's needs, you are a consultant discovering how your company can best serve those needs. Consider how you feel and act at this stage of the sales process.

- Are you relaxed when you ask questions?
- While the buyer answers your questions, do you fidget in anticipation of what you will say next?

- At the first mention of a need, are you ready to interrupt the buyer to provide a solution?
- Do you ask questions too quickly, like the *rat-tat-tat* of machine gun fire?

If you immediately ask one question after another, the buyer may feel as if she is being interrogated—sort of like what we just did with the above questions.

A conversation is an oral exchange of sentiments, observations, opinions, or ideas. In sales, this definition includes information. It's wise to allow a brief moment between your questions to show that you are giving serious consideration to the information the buyer has provided.

b. Reflective listening encourages additional conversation

Reflective listening is a natural activity when you are speaking with friends and family. It involves the nonverbal listening skills mentioned above as well as verbal encouragements such as:

"Really?"
"Tell me more."
"Wow!"
"Then what happened?"

As the buyer answers your questions and provides valuable information to help you make the sale, give her your feedback about what she is saying. That demonstrates you are actively listening, and it encourages her to continue talking.

For example, listen to how a television or radio talk show host encourages his guests to talk. He does not interview his guests like a news reporter, drilling them with one sharp or curt informational question after another. Rather, the talk show host encourages relaxed yet lively conversations fueled by open-ended questions and reflective listening.

One of the subtle tools to accomplish this is to ask reflective questions that repeat what was just said. The buyer says, "I'm not sure if we will do anything this year with such a tight budget!" The salesperson responds, "You're uncertain as to how you'll work within your budget?"

That's a reflective question. The salesperson changed the buyer's words a bit, but the question reflects back to the buyer the essence of what was just said. It demonstrates to the buyer that she has been heard.

To help you remember, this questioning technique is also called the *porcupine* questioning technique. If someone tossed a porcupine into your lap, wouldn't your initial reaction be to toss it back? Say a potential client asks, "How long does it take to get this product delivered?" Rather than give a straight-up answer like "Three days," just gently toss the question back to gain more information. You may say, "What time frame would be acceptable for your needs?"

For example, if it turns out this buyer needs inventory in two days, you've just made it more difficult to close the sale by saying you need three days. In contrast, if he says, "We need it in ten days," then you would look like a hero by telling him that your standard delivery time frame is only three days.

Note: It may sound odd if you ask a reflective question ten times in a row. Obviously, frequent use of any strategy will make the buyer feel uncomfortable and start to wonder if you're using strategies or psychology on them. The buyer will immediately raise defense barriers. Use your common sense regarding the frequency of reflective questions. Used sparingly, reflective questions can be an effective tool for encouraging buyers to share important information.

When the buyer mentions a need that you want to learn more about, reflect the essence of what he just said, and do so with a similar energy level. Then remain silent until the buyer speaks. When you maintain a listening posture, the buyer will take your cue and often keep on talking.

Exercise in listening skills

Let's put your listening skills into action. Below are three of the questions listed earlier in the chapter. Each question is followed by four common types of responses.

Example #1

Salesperson: *"What are the biggest challenges you face regarding your industry?"*
Buyer: *"Getting our suppliers to deliver when they promise they will."*

Which response is closest to what you would say next?

A. "We provide overnight shipping to make sure that you will always receive our product when you need it."
B. "When is your busiest time of year?"
C. "What time frames do you need for timely delivery? Over-night? Weekly?"
D. "Your suppliers don't deliver when they promise?"

In response A, the salesperson responded to the buyer's need by beginning to sell immediately. At first glance, this response may seem like the best course of action. A need was identified, and the salesperson began selling.

In response B, the salesperson moved on to an unrelated question. The salesperson asked a question and received some good information. Task completed. Now ask the next question. Could the salesperson have stayed on the subject a bit longer and learned some additional valuable information? Probably.

In response C, the salesperson listened, and based on the content of the buyer's answer, asked a more specific open-ended question. In other words, "Tell me a bit more about this one aspect of your answer." The advantage of asking a deeper question is that the salesperson can use the additional information learned to give a more persuasive presentation and a more compelling close. The salesperson accomplishes this by explaining how the company's business model is structured to make sure the buyer will receive products in the desired time frame.

In response D, the salesperson reflected back the essence of what the buyer just said. This response will not direct the buyer's attention to any specific aspect of his answer. Instead, it simply gives permission for the buyer to continue talking. This type of response is very useful if the buyer is passionate about his previous response. When the buyer is worked up about a topic, let him air out his passion. You can redirect the conversation with more specific questions a few minutes later.

Notice that in the last two replies, the salesperson *did not* begin selling right away. There is plenty of time for selling during the presentation. When the buyer presents a need, find out as much as possible about the need so you can sell more persuasively when the time comes.

Example #2

Salesperson: *"When is your busiest time of year?"*
Buyer: *"During the summer months and the holidays between Thanksgiving and Christmas."*

Which response is closest to what you would say next?

A. "What are your business objectives for this year?"
B. "The summer months are some of your busiest?"

C. "We keep the largest inventory during the summer months to make sure our customers always have product when they need it most."

D. "What type of supply issues do you experience during your busy summer months?"

In response A, the salesperson decided not to gather any more information about the buyer's busy season and moved on to the next topic.

In response B, the salesperson reflected back what the buyer just said. This opened the door for the buyer to give additional information about the busy summer season.

In response C, the salesperson heard the buyer identify her busy season. Assuming that lack of inventory was a problem, the salesperson immediately began selling, explaining why his company delivers great customer service during the buyer's busy season. It is a powerful selling point…unless supply is not the buyer's primary concern.

In response D, the salesperson, based on the content of the buyer's reply, asked a more specific open-ended question. This allows the salesperson to discover if product supply is a key element in the decision to consider switching to another provider. If it is not a key issue, the salesperson can downplay or eliminate that topic during the presentation. The open-ended question encourages the buyer to disclose other types of issues that she experiences during the busy season. That's always a good idea.

Example #3

In this example, you get to lead the discussion. Show your mastery of this topic by filling in examples of the four types of responses:

Salesperson: *"How does your company make decisions about new purchases?"*

Buyer: *"I run everything past my manager, who checks the annual budget."*

Now give an example of each response:

A. Reflect what the buyer just said.
B. Start selling.
C. Based on that reply, ask a more specific open-ended question.
D. Move on to the next topic.

In response A, did you reflect what the buyer said with a response similar to "You and your manager work together to make decisions about new purchases?"

In response B, did you start selling with a response similar to "Our website gives you access to all purchases year-to-date, so your manager will know exactly where you stand as to the budget!"

In response C, did you ask a more specific question based on the buyer's response? For example, "How often do you and your manager meet to discuss purchasing decisions of this nature?"

In response D, it is easy to change the subject—especially when you aren't paying much attention and plan to give the same basic presentation regardless of the buyer's response. When you listen to the buyer and respond accordingly, you stand out from the wait-and-see competition.

Asking reflective questions or specific open-ended questions based on the buyer's reply often gathers additional valuable information to close the sale.

c. Take notes

During face-to-face sales appointments, you can set yourself apart from the competition by occasionally taking notes about important information buyers share with you. You can use a legal pad, a spiral binder, or a laptop or tablet. Avoid taking notes on your smartphone without telling buyers what you're doing, as it can appear you are texting rather than listening.

Two suggestions for taking notes:

1. Don't make a big deal out of taking notes. "Well, let me open up my business binder and take some notes to show you how much I value your every word!" No salesperson would actually say that, but you can imply that by your actions if you make a big show of getting out whatever you will use to take your notes.

2. Write down *only* the key points. You are a consultant, not a reporter interviewing someone for a front-page story. When the buyer says something significant, make a quick note of it. If the buyer begins describing specific challenges, your written notes may increase.

Another important reason to take notes is so you can remember what the buyers said. As a busy salesperson, your thoughts are filled with a dozen tasks pulling at your attention. If you see ten or more buyers each week, how will you remember which buyer said what without taking notes? Relying on your memory is a sure way to lose or confuse information. We agree with the Chinese proverb that states: *The faintest ink is better than the greatest memory.*

d. Don't interrupt

This final point should be most obvious, yet it is frequently ignored. Why would salespeople interrupt a buyer who is providing valuable information that can be used to close the sale? Here are two reasons. Hopefully they're not yours.

1. Poor listening habits. Do you habitually interrupt people anytime you think of something to say? Ask your friends, family, and work colleagues. If you discover that you often interrupt people as they speak, please stop. Interrupting others is bad for business and bad for your personal relationships. Such interruptions also ruin any sense of rapport you have built with your buyer.

2. Unbridled enthusiasm. Does a buying signal spoken by a buyer create in you an irresistible urge to immediately start selling? The buyer says, "You know, the owner and I were just talking about getting a product of this type…" and you blurt out, "…and if you buy this month, you get 10 percent off!"

Enthusiasm is a selling asset, but it must be controlled. If you immediately jump on every buying signal, you will annoy buyers with your rude interruptions, decrease the rapport you established, and miss key additional information that could be necessary for closing the sale that day.

For instance, if the salesperson had not interrupted, the buyer might have added a qualifier to the buying signal: "The owner and I were just talking about getting a product of this type. He wants to wait a couple of months to make a purchase—until after tax season."

That extra information changes the dynamics of your presentation. By listening a moment longer, you can learn that to close the sale that day, you must emphasize the advantages of acting now and the disadvantages of waiting. By continuing to ask additional open-ended questions, you may learn more about why the owner wants to wait. Perhaps the owner is worried about paying a large amount of money in taxes. Perhaps the owner is selling another property and funds will be tight until the sale is finalized. Perhaps the owner is waiting until the busy season begins in order to determine the amount of cash flow available for the purchase. In short, keep your enthusiasm under control.

When you discover the answers to those questions before the presentation, you can shape your presentation to avoid unnecessary resistance at the close.

Buyers often feel compelled to defend concerns they raise *after* a presentation, because that is their response to your request for immediate action. You'll likely hear "yes, but" from them as you address their concerns and risk falling into an "I'm right and you're wrong" scenario. Surprisingly, when buyers state those very same concerns *before* the presentation, they do not feel compelled to defend them, because they are merely answering your discovery questions. By letting your buyers state as many of their concerns as possible *before* you start the presentation, you can direct the course of your presentation to keep clear the path to a closed sale.

Habitually interrupting buyers dooms you to delivering one-size-fits-all presentations that do not specifically address the needs of each buyer. You have probably delivered one-size-fits-all presentations in the past because you did not discover the buying dynamics required to close the sale. That is wait-and-see selling. It is the difference between an effective *presentation* and a sales *pitch*. It is the difference between a top sales professional and an average salesperson. Buyers will always be less persuaded by generic presentations. Have you been delivering them?

CHAPTER 7 KEY POINTS

- Know how to develop and use a transition strategy to move the conversation from small talk to business.
- If you ask questions but fail to show the buyer that you are listening to her answers, your questions will do little to help you close the sale.
- Closed-ended questions elicit one-word answers that effectively shut down your sales presentation.

- Open-ended questions require thought and elaboration from your buyer.
- Always use nonverbal cues to show that you are listening.
- Set yourself apart from the competition by taking an appropriate amount of notes.
- Enthusiasm is a selling asset, but it must be controlled.

8. Discovery Questions

Everything you say or do during your sales appointment should be done to move your buyer one step closer to taking immediate action. In fact, the purpose of your carefully thought-out questions is always to keep the sale moving toward the close.

Remember, open-ended questions will elicit much of the vital information you need in order to close the sale by the end of the sales appointment. If your open-ended questions do not elicit enough of the specific information you need to close the sale, it is advantageous to ask a specific set of questions called *discovery questions*. These questions are designed to get buyers to tell you specifically more about their process and expectations related to owning your product.

There are four basic discovery questions. They are universal questions that address the most common concerns possible in every sales appointment, regardless of your industry or profession. Your goal is to craft them in such a way that they fit seamlessly into your conversations with buyers. Depending on your industry, there may also be one or two industry-specific discovery questions you will need to ask.

For example, if you are a real estate agent talking to a buyer who wants to purchase a home, an important discovery question is, "Are you working with another real estate agent?" If you fail to discover that the buyer is working with another agent, the buyer may use your time and gas to find a home that the other agent will sell him!

If you are an account manager for one of the trades, and you are talking to a building owner about a maintenance agreement for their HVAC system or their elevators, an important discovery question is, "When does your current maintenance agreement expire?" Without this information, you may invest your company's resources to survey that building's equipment only to discover the building owner is not able to make an agreement with your company for several more years.

AVOID SURPRISES

The main purpose of discovery questions is to eliminate avoidable surprises at the close. Every common question or concern not discovered before the presentation can become a potential challenge to the sale later on. If you leave the discovery of the common concerns until after the presentation, you increase the probability of being surprised by concerns you may have avoided had you addressed them earlier. The sales process has enough surprises without you unnecessarily creating more. Discovery questions prevent this by uncovering the common, reoccurring concerns early in the sales process.

THE FOUR DISCOVERY QUESTIONS

Discovery Question #1: "Who makes the final decision?"

The potential objection at the close is for a buyer to simply say, "Well, I don't make the final decision." The sales pitfall is trying to get a non–decision maker to make a buying decision during the sales appointment. Another way to word the first discovery question is, "Who, other than yourself, might be involved in making the final decision?"

What are the advantages of discovering who makes the buying decision before you begin your presentation?

95

1. You don't waste anyone's time—yours or that of the person you've been speaking with. When you discover that the person you've been speaking with is not the decision maker, give only enough of a presentation to prove that you should be given the opportunity to address the real decision maker.

2. You can make arrangements to include the real decision maker in your presentation.

The wording of your request to meet with the ultimate decision maker will influence the answer you get from the non–decision maker. For example, if you ask, "Can I meet with the owner?" then you have asked a closed question that elicits a *yes/no* answer. This question assumes that meeting the owner may not be a possibility. The closed-ended format makes it easy for the gate-keeper to say *no*. However, the same question asked as an open-ended question creates a different expectation:

- "When can I meet with the owner?"
- "What is the procedure for arranging a meeting with the owner?"
- "How can I schedule a meeting with the owner?"

Each of those open-ended questions assumes that a meeting with the owner is possible. That *positive* assumption increases the probability of a favorable response. Even if you do not receive a favorable response, the open-ended format of the question will elicit more information than a *yes* or *no* answer. That additional information may also create another possibility for accessing the decision maker. For example, the gatekeeper may answer, "No, the owner lives out of town."

But at least now you have additional key information about the owner, and you can suggest alternative formats for a meeting.

- "When is the best time to arrange a conference call with the owner?"
- "How often is the owner in town?"
- "What is the procedure for arranging a meeting when the owner is in town?"

TRAIN YOUR GATEKEEPER TO BECOME YOUR SALESPERSON

How do you respond if you have no direct access to the decision maker? The gatekeeper says, "The owner pays me to screen all the vendors. I will take your information to the decision maker and present it together with all the other vendor proposals."

In this scenario, your rapport with the gatekeeper becomes increasingly important. People like to do business with people they like! You are at the mercy of how the gatekeeper presents your proposal, so it always pays to maintain and deepen your rapport with the gatekeeper.

If you discover that the gatekeeper is not the decision maker before the presentation begins, then you can use your presentation to train the gatekeeper to become, in effect, your salesperson. You cover the same content in your presentation, but you address the gatekeeper as your presenter. When you treat gatekeepers with respect, they will be more relaxed and will retain more of the key information you want given to the decision maker.

1. Keep it simple. The gatekeeper will not remember ten benefits of your product when presenting your information to the decision maker. The gatekeeper will remember only two or three key benefits at the most, so during your presentation emphasize the two or three most important points. Ask questions to determine which challenges weigh heaviest in the decision maker's desire to find a solution. Also ask which

other vendors are presenting solutions. In many cases, companies do not mind sharing that information, and you, as a true sales professional, will know the strengths and weaknesses of your competition and be able to address them in your proposal.

2. Have literature available for the gatekeeper to pass on to the decision maker. If appropriate, offer to prepare an introductory letter with the basic points of your presentation. This letter will equip the gatekeeper with a clear outline to follow when discussing your product with the decision maker. List your most persuasive benefits first, and keep the letter as short as possible. No need to give the gatekeeper a lot of copy to read.

3. The final option is to figure out how to go around the gatekeeper and approach the decision maker directly. This may be prudent *only* as a last resort, when all other actions have failed and you have nothing to lose. Otherwise, it is generally not a good strategy, because it will adversely affect your relationship with the gatekeeper, with whom you may need to work in the future. It is generally best to work within the system of the gatekeeper's company whenever possible. It is better for the long-term business relationship with the decision maker, and it is better for generating referrals. In the final chapter of this book, we will explore the process of developing referrals.

Notice how this first discovery question helps you avoid one of the procrastination objections, "I have to check with someone else for approval." By discovering the answer to this discovery question *before* your presentation begins, you will rarely be surprised at the close with "I don't make the buying decision," because the buyer will tell you early in your meeting whether or not she is the sole decision maker.

Discovery Question #2: "When does the decision maker plan to take action?" Or, "How soon do you need to have the best solution in place?"

This second discovery question addresses that frequent and nebulous potential objection, "I want to think about it." If you already know when they need to have a solution, you'll know when the order will have to be placed in order to meet that need. The answer to this question can really help you to create a sense of urgency for the buyer to make a decision today.

Is it possible to talk to a buyer who is the sole decision maker, but the buyer still can't make the decision until a later time? Yes.

- Perhaps the buyer is waiting for money. The source could be from a tax return, a settlement of some sort, or a sales report that impacts the budget.
- Perhaps the buyer is leaving town or is about to take an extended leave from the business.
- Perhaps the manager who oversees the purchase just resigned, and the buyer must fill that vacant position before making the purchase.
- Perhaps the buyer makes a habit of gaining feedback from the end users of the product and wants to wait until he can present multiple options for consideration.

If you discover that the buyer plans to make a buying decision weeks or months after your sales appointment, then during your presentation you can emphasize the benefits of taking action immediately and the consequences of procrastinating. Make sure you understand the reasons the buyer is delaying his decision so you can present reasonable alternatives for him to take immediate action.

For example, if the delay is due to finances, perhaps the buyer can split the investment into smaller, more manageable amounts, or he can use a credit card. Perhaps the buyer can lock in the total amount at a lower rate now by endorsing an agreement with a small initial investment.

If you cannot overcome a delayed buying decision during your presentation, discover when the buyer *can* make a decision, and secure an agreement on the next step of your follow-up before you leave the sales appointment. You may not win the sale today, but you may be able to lock out any competitors when the time is right for the buyer to make a final decision.

Discovery Question #3: "If you decide to invest in the product, are the funds available for you to move forward today?" Or, "If everything we discuss now points to my product being the best solution for your current needs, is there anything standing in the way of you making a decision today?"

The potential objection is the buyer saying, "I don't have the money right now to pay for your product." You want to avoid giving a presentation that attempts to close now when the buyer's funds won't be available until later.

Please note that this discovery question addresses the buyer's ability to purchase your product, *not the price* of your product. If the buyer has no available funds to purchase your product, how can she take immediate action at the close? This discovery question is somewhat related to Discovery Question #2 above, because it inquires about the *when* of the availability of the buyer's money.

If you discover that funding is a challenge before you start the presentation, then during the presentation you can focus on the financing possibilities available to the buyer. For example, if the buyer says, "The funds won't be available for at least six months," what options can you explore?

Your follow-up questions will depend on your industry or profession. Possibilities may include:

- "Would it help if we broke the amount into several smaller pieces?"
- "Could you use a credit card or get a short-term loan?"
- "Would you be interested in learning about our company's finance plan?"

If you cannot work out a solution for the buyer to take immediate action, confirm when the funding will be available, then try to secure an agreement on the next step of your follow-up before you leave the sales appointment.

Discovery Question #4: "Is price your only consideration, or is quality also important?"

The potential objection is, "This costs too much." The sales pitfall is attempting to compete on price with price-based competition if your company offers a *value-based* proposition.

It is important to understand which type of money questions buyers have. Otherwise, you may unnecessarily give away profit margin. At the close, you ask the buyer to take immediate action and the buyer says, "I'm not sure about the money."

You immediately reply, "If you act now, I'll give you a 10 percent discount!"

The buyer's face brightens. "Thanks for the discount, but my question wasn't about price. It's about cash flow. I don't have the cash right now to buy your product."

Oops.

If you confuse price questions with funding questions, you may unnecessarily give a reduction in the amount when the buyer was actually asking about funding options. That is a costly mistake!

You will notice that the final discovery question is an either/or question. Closed-ended questions can be appropriate for eliciting a precise answer here.

Note: The warning given in chapter 7 about asking closed-ended questions refers to questions asked early in the sales appointment, when you are encouraging buyers to engage in conversation.

At this point in the sales appointment, you are nearing the start of your presentation. You need this specific information to present solutions more persuasively. So using a closed-ended question is the appropriate tool for efficiently gathering that information.

The fourth discovery question asks if the top priority for the decision maker is finding the lowest amount. The either/or format provides buyers with a clear choice—is the lowest amount the top priority regardless of quality, or is quality also an important consideration?

This discovery question takes us to the heart of persuasion. There are two basic types of sales scenarios: selling price and selling value.

1. When selling price, the salesperson says, "You should buy from me because my product has the lowest price."
2. When selling value, the salesperson says, "My product gives you the best value for your money."

Your company's products or services can have degrees of both elements. The critical question is whether you are *primarily* selling the lowest price or the best value for the buyer's money.

Because of the either/or format of this discovery question, buyers will frequently give you one of two answers. Some buyers will reply, "It's all about price. I'm only interested in the lowest price you can offer." When that is the reply, you must adjust your presentation to:

- offer a competitive investment,
- explain how your higher investment is actually competitive, if it's not blatantly obvious (for example, your product is concentrated or includes features that the competition charges extra for), or
- persuade buyers that quality is a far more important consideration than the money (for example, the cheapest products on the market must be replaced again in five years).

Other buyers will give a mixed answer like "Quality is important to us. But we want a good price, too." If you sell a value-based product, that is the type of reply you want to hear. That answer opens the door for you to explain how value and price come together in your product.

Bear in mind that the key to a profitable sales career is asking questions. Not just any questions, but the questions that provide you with the information required to close the sale that day. In a multicall environment, your questions will identify the buyer's purchasing process more clearly and move the sale forward during each contact. When you have discovered the following:

- who makes the buying decision,
- when a decision can be made,
- when the funds for the purchase will be available, and
- if the buyer is primarily motivated by price or value,

then you are ready to give a persuasive presentation that is truly tailored to the individual buying dynamics.

What follows are the continuations of our selling scenarios that highlight the strategies presented in this chapter.

Scenario 1: Business Sales Appointment

Kate has established sufficient rapport with Mr. Stevens. Now she is ready to shift the conversation to business and gather the information she needs to provide a compelling, relevant presentation. Her objective is to connect the past business experiences Mr. Stevens mentioned during their rapport-building small talk to his current business challenges. Kate begins with a transition question: "So how did you get started using widgets?"

Mr. Stevens tells her about a past work situation where his team encountered a challenge. They used a widget as a solution, and his teams have used them ever since. That opens the door to her follow-up, open-ended questions:

"How are your employees using widgets in the field now?"
"What are some of the challenges that they face with your current widgets?"
"How is the service with your current widget service provider?"
"What are some ways your current widgets could be improved?"

Kate opens her presentation folder and jots down several notes about the situations he mentions where her widgets would excel over his current widgets. She will refer to those key notes during her presentation.

What type of information do your potential clients provide that is worthy of noting in writing?

While asking these questions, Kate works into their conversation several discovery questions to confirm his buying dynamics. She guesses Mr. Stevens is a sole proprietor, but she asks the *who* discovery question to confirm that he is, in fact, the only decision maker: "Dean, when it comes to business decisions about matters like widgets, do you make the final decision, or are other people involved?"

"Well, I like to consult with the men in the field, because they use the widgets all day long," Mr. Stevens replies. "But ultimately, I am the one who decides."

His answer confirms what Kate suspected—that Mr. Stevens is the primary decision maker. Her excitement increases. First, he is facing ongoing challenges that Widget Corp could clearly address. Second, he is capable of making a buying decision by himself.

Next, she decides to ask the *when* discovery question: "You had mentioned some challenges with your current widget. When does your current service agreement expire?"

"We opted out of our current provider's annual contract last year. Right now, we are on a month-to-month service plan," Mr. Stevens says.

That's the type of answer Kate wants to hear. She asks one additional question to confirm that he is free to make a decision today: "So if you see some options that are more advantageous to your company, you are free to make a change whenever you choose?"

"That is correct," Mr. Stevens replies.

What type of information do your potential clients provide that tempts you to begin selling immediately rather than continuing to gather more information?

From the way Mr. Stevens discusses the busy schedules of his work teams, it appears that his business is prospering.

However, Kate knows that a busy business is not necessarily a profitable business. Kate asks the *funding* discovery question to confirm that he is financially able to make a buying decision: "And if you decide to make a change, are the funds available now for you to take action?"

"We have monies budgeted for this sort of thing," Mr. Stevens says, letting her know that his business is doing well. He also wants her to know he is a patient buyer. "But right now, we're making do with what we've got."

"I understand. I would like to talk more about your current equipment, but first, I have one last question." Kate knows that she is competing against a price-driven, small local company, so she asks the *price* discovery question: "Is price the major driver in your decision about widgets, or is quality also important?"

Mr. Stevens leans back in his chair. "We're always on the lookout for the best deal, but recently, we've had some delays because of our current widgets." He shakes his head. "I don't know. It's starting to cost us money."

Kate likes all of his answers so far, and she believes the sales appointment is progressing nicely.

- She established herself as a serious businessperson.
- She built a professional level of rapport.
- Mr. Stevens is responding to her questions and is slowly revealing his dissatisfaction with his current widget provider.
- Kate discovered his buying dynamics and has several examples from his business experiences to reference during her presentation.

She is now ready to start presenting solutions. Kate pulls a tablet from her bag and begins...

Scenario 2: Residential Sales Appointment

Bob established sufficient rapport with Gary and Pat by discussing subjects of general interest, their home and family. Now he transitions to subjects related to business to identify Pat and Gary's needs for a widget. Bob asks, "What will those changes mean for both of you when Diane eventually moves out of the house?"

Gary and Pat look earnestly at each other and begin sharing the changes they see ahead. Bob listens, taking mental notes as Gary and Pat explain the needs that a widget could address. Reflectively listening, Bob encourages them to continue talking with reflective questions:

"Really, that much?"
"By bad service, you mean...?"
"Wow. They said that?"
"What will happen after that?"

Bob moves the conversation toward their unique circumstances by interspersing reflective questions that are more industry specific:

"What type of needs do you believe a widget will help address?"
"What has been your experience with widgets so far?"

While answering these questions, Gary and Pat mention a few concerns they have about the widget industry. Bob is not ready to start his presentation yet, so he responds with, "Those are frequently asked questions that I will address in just a few minutes."

To encourage Pat and Gary to continue talking about their needs, he asks his next question: "You were talking about your experience with widgets. What are your thoughts about…?"

How do you keep potential clients focused on your questions that identify their needs when they ask questions about information you plan to address later during the presentation?

After several minutes of listening, Bob has now heard Pat and Gary's answers to his industry-specific questions. He has a good idea about Pat and Gary's starting point concerning widgets. Bob has made several mental notes about their concerns, and he plans to specifically address those concerns during his presentation.

Bob is almost ready to start his presentation. But first, he wants to discover Pat and Gary's buying dynamics by working the four discovery questions into the conversation. He begins with the *who* question, identifying who is involved in the decision-making process: "As you know, a widget affects the entire family to some degree. To make sure I understand correctly, will the two of you make this decision, or will other family members be involved?"

Pat responds quickly. "Oh, no. The two of us will decide what we want to do." Bob glances at Gary, who nods in agreement.

Bob continues with the *when* discovery question: "A few minutes ago, you mentioned your interest in a widget. Generally speaking, what was the time frame you had in mind? Were you thinking weeks, months…years?"

They both laugh at the idea of years. Gary says, "Well, our daughter will graduate from college at the end of next year, but we don't want to wait until then. If we found a good deal, it would be sooner rather than later."

Bob wants to narrow down the time frame a bit more to avoid any procrastination excuses that might come later in the sales appointment. "So by sooner, do you mean in a few days? A few weeks?"

Pat and Gary look at each other. Gary shrugs. "If it is a good deal, we might be ready sometime this month."

How do you respond when potential clients do not directly answer your key questions?

Bob weighs their answers. He asked twice. They didn't use the exact words, but they *seem* to be able to make a decision that evening. So far, Bob has confirmed that he is speaking to the decision makers and they may be ready to make an immediate decision. Next, Bob asks the *funding* discovery question to see if they have the funds to act on their decision: "Thank you for sharing that. If you see a widget that meets all the needs and conditions you have in mind, are the funds available now to take action on it?"

Gary quickly replies, "Well, it depends on the widget."

"Certainly," Bob agrees. "We'll get into all of that in a minute. But if you see a widget that is just what you and Pat want, do you have the funds available to move forward?"

Bob words the question vaguely so that answering it does

not seem like a commitment to buy. Bob is not asking them to buy. He simply wants to know if they have enough funds in the bank to buy a widget. If they answer yes, then he knows that one less obstacle lies between the potential clients and a buying decision that evening. If they say no, then he will talk in depth about the Residential Widgets finance plan during his presentation.

Gary casts a glance at Pat and shrugs again. "Yeah, if it's a widget that we like."

"Fair enough," Bob says. He moves on to the *price* discovery question: "Pat, earlier you mentioned your thoughts about pricing. Let me ask both of you, is lowest price your only concern, or is quality also an important consideration?"

"Well…" They both chime out in unison and stop short. Pat finishes their response: "Price is important, but we want something of quality that we can be proud of."

"Agreed," Gary adds. "This is too much money to waste on junk that doesn't perform as promised."

Bob nods in acknowledgment. He has accomplished his prepresentation objectives:

- He established a comfortable rapport with Gary and Pat. Both of them are engaged and participating in the conversation.
- They expressed some concerns about the widget industry, so Bob knows he must spend time in his presentation specifically addressing those concerns.
- Bob also discovered Pat and Gary's buying dynamics: they are the sole decision makers.
- They can probably make a decision now, but he sensed some hesitation.

- They have the funds to purchase a widget.
- They are open to considering a value-based widget rather than simply the lowest-priced widget.

How do *you* decide when it is time to start the presentation?

Bob opens his presentation notebook. Now he is ready to start the presentation...

CHAPTER 8 KEY POINTS

- The main purpose of discovery questions is to eliminate avoidable surprises at the close.
- When gatekeepers prevent you from meeting directly with the decision makers, it's in your best interest to train the gatekeeper to become your salesperson.
- When potential clients are not able to make an immediate buying decision or do not have the funding available, ask follow-up questions that explore options that may allow them to take action that day.
- The answers to your discovery questions will help you determine what solutions to present that will be most compelling to each buyer.

9. Lowering the Buyer's Resistance during Your Presentation

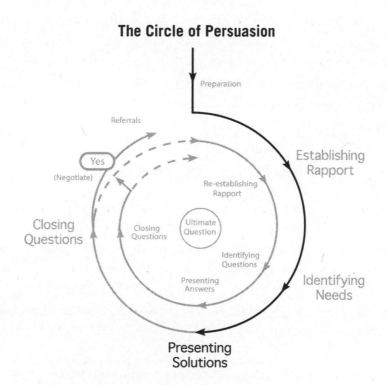

The Circle of Persuasion

Preparation

Referrals

Yes

(Negotiate)

Re-establishing Rapport

Establishing Rapport

Closing Questions

Closing Questions

Ultimate Question

Identifying Questions

Presenting Answers

Identifying Needs

Presenting Solutions

Now that you have established rapport and learned what the buyer wants and needs through your discovery questions, it's time to present your product in such a way as to gradually lower sales resistance and to increase sales acceptance.

There is a common belief that education is all it takes for buyers to make buying decisions. This belief originates from the assumption that education equals persuasion. If you educate clients enough, they will buy.

But is that always true? Have you ever felt that you educated potential clients on all the benefits of buying your product...and they agreed with your presentation...but then they didn't buy?

The truth is that the worst consequence of the assumption that education equals persuasion is the tendency for salespeople to breathe sighs of relief after finishing the presentation and think, *My main work is now done. I've enthusiastically presented the potential client with reasons to buy. Now I will answer any questions and see what the buyer does next.* That is an example of wait-and-see selling. And you don't want to be in that predicament.

WHAT IS A PRESENTATION?

A presentation is where information is exchanged. As you give information, you request and receive feedback. The feedback received is information that points you in the direction you must take next in order to gain and keep satisfied clients.

You give dozens of presentations each business week. Here are some examples of presentations that you may not have previously considered presentations:

• *Answering questions:* A client calls you with a question about using your product. Rather than simply answering the client's question and ending the call, you see the opportunity to subtly remind him that your availability and helpfulness in answering his questions is an example of the exceptional customer service you promised during your initial presentation, when he decided to purchase the product.

- *Problem solving:* Your client has ongoing performance challenges with a product. During the conversation about resolving the issue, you can introduce the possibility of investing in a newer or higher-grade model that will provide the stepped-up performance your client now needs.

- *Customer service:* You call a client with an update that a recent order is now on the way. This is an opportunity to present to your client that you truly care about the level of service she receives—that you are your client's advocate inside the company. Each communication with your clients or potential clients should be considered an active presentation for reselling them on your brand and on you as a sales professional.

PRESENTATION SKILLS

While the content of your presentation will be specific to your industry, there are common strategies to increase the persuasiveness of any presentation. When you make presentations, your nonverbal behaviors continue to speak louder than words. We will cover both audio and visual components of making presentations. Then we will discuss several powerful concepts that transform sales presentations into persuasive calls to action.

1. Assumptive tone of voice

An assumptive tone of voice is your most powerful, persuasive weapon. Always talk about your product or service with the same confidence you would have in saying that the sun rises in the east every morning and sets in the west each evening. Use the same tonality that you would use to state that the Earth is round. In other words, make sure that your statements sound like definitive and confident statements, not questions.

Sometimes a salesperson will raise the pitch of her voice at the end of statements so it sounds like she is asking a question. Her intention is to state a fact: "We provide great service." But because the pitch of her voice rises at the end of the sentence, the buyer hears her say, "We provide great service?"

A questioning tone does not convey conviction. Ending anything but the final closing sentence with a question will decrease your closing ratio, because potential clients buy assurance, not doubts.

An assumptive tonality ends sentences with a slightly lower pitch. Try this: Make an audio recording of yourself making statements you believe are obviously true—statements everyone knows are true. Do you hear the certainty in your voice? Listen to other people who speak confidently about any subject. What do they do with their voices to create a sense of certainty? Within the natural range of your voice and personality, emulate aspects of their tonality to add confidence to your voice.

2. Questions versus statements

Whenever appropriate during your presentations, ask questions rather than making statements. Most of your questions will be rhetorical ones that do not require a verbal response. Nonetheless, your questions will engage the participation of your listeners on a mental level. The general rule in sales is that a participating listener is a buying listener.

Questions require listeners to think and respond. When listeners mentally respond to your questions, it's important to remember that their answers are from their perspective and expressed in their mental voice, rather than your words spoken in your external voice.

Many salespeople think that persuasive selling is all about making statements. The fact is that when buyers listen to your external voice, they have an *internal* conversation about what they are hearing you say. Their internal conversation—not your statements—is what convinces potential clients to take action.

If the buyer is thinking *price, price, price,* and you ask how important quality is to him, the buyer must process the idea of quality just to understand your question. The concept of quality may not have been in his thoughts before you mentioned it. Just the idea that he is now processing the concept of quality is a huge win for you. It has reoriented the buyer's thoughts toward your value proposition. It doesn't mean you've closed the sale, but it does mean you are better positioned to close the sale.

To paraphrase an old saying, if they chew on it long enough, eventually they may swallow it. The purpose of the presentation is to get potential clients chewing on the idea of owning your product.

Continuing the example above, consider the impact of introducing the importance of quality in the form of a question. The buyer will not only briefly consider the concept of quality, but because you have introduced that question, he will also consider the answer to your question.

If you simply make a statement such as "Quality is important," the buyer may passively listen to that statement as he does to the many other statements of the presentation. When you ask a question such as "How will the quality of this product affect the value you would receive from it?" which requires more than a *yes* or *no* answer, he will hear his answer in his internal voice. You have influenced the buyer on a deeper level, because you engaged his thoughts on a topic of your choosing. *The theory here is that if you say something, the buyer may doubt it. If the buyer says something, it must be true.*

Does that mean we can control buyers' internal conversations or conclusions? No. The best we can do is influence the direction of their thoughts. By understanding how the form of what we say affects the thought processes of our buyers, we can introduce our selling concepts in a manner that allows us to be most persuasive on the deepest level.

3. Say what you want them to do

When you are presenting to buyers, whether making statements or asking questions, absolutely say what you want buyers to do, not what you don't want them to do.

If you say, "Imagine a bright, sunny day," then to follow your statement the buyer must make a mental image of a bright, sunny day. It may not be the same image of a sunny day that you have in mind. The image may last for only a split second, but on some level the buyer will briefly make a mental image of a bright, sunny day to understand what you just said.

Now here is the tricky part. If you say, "Don't imagine a bright sunny day," then on some level of thought, the buyer must still make a mental image of a bright, sunny day to make sense of what not to imagine. The lesson: if you say it, the buyer must process it in a mental picture.

Always say what you want buyers to do, not what you don't want them to do. Avoid action verbs that paint mental pictures of buyers doing the opposite of what you want them to do. Do not use words like:

- *hesitate*
- *think about*
- *fear*
- *wait/delay*
- *worry*

These words introduce into the minds of potential clients images that are the opposite of what you will ask them to do at the close.

4. Key word patterns

The type of wording people use reflects their mental processes for making buying decisions. By wording your presentation to align with the words that buyers habitually use, you will find another way to be like them, deepen your rapport, and lower sales resistance. More important, you will not break rapport with them by using wording that reflects a type of thinking very different from theirs.

Once again, this is a penalty situation. Just because your words match the buyer's type of thinking, it does not mean she will buy from you. But if your words are very different from hers, that difference can create a discomfort that can negatively affect the rapport you've built.

There is an additional element in this wording that is subtle yet noticeable. The first two word patterns below have a motivational element to them. By aligning your words with the way your buyers think, you provide motivation for them to take positive action. Likewise, if your wording goes against how they think, it can contribute to the buyers' inaction.

Here are some examples.

1. *Want/avoid*

Some buyers talk about the good things they *want* to have happen.

- They *want* the product to be shipped on time.
- They *want* the product to work reliably.
- They *want* the product to make their lives more enjoyable.

Other buyers talk about the bad things they want to *avoid*.

- They *don't want* the product to arrive late.
- They *don't want* the product to stop working.
- They *don't want* the product to make their lives miserable.

119

In those examples, the buyers are actually talking about the same subject, but their focus is completely different.

Note: This isn't either/or thinking. Avoid the tendency to put buyers into boxes by saying, "Potential client A is a Want Person. Potential client B is an Avoid Person."

Instead, imagine a sliding scale with "want" at one extreme and "avoid" at the other. People fall somewhere between those two extremes. Some buyers do not have strong tendencies in using one type of word pattern. They use a mixture. Other buyers will constantly use one type of wording or the other. Those are the buyers you want to become aware of. The more that buyers use one type of word pattern, the more important it is that you do not use the opposite type of wording.

---

2. *Can/must*

Some buyers talk in terms of what they *can* do. They use possibility-driven words like *can, could,* and *want.*

"I can check with the boss for approval."
"We could probably use the company credit card for this purchase."
"We want to figure out how we can make this purchase fit in the budget."

Other buyers talk in terms of what they *must* do. They use necessity-driven words such as *must, need to, have to, should,* and *would.*

"I must wait until my tax refund check arrives."
"I need to talk with my spouse first."

"I have to wait until the kids get out of school."
"I should hold off on further spending until..."
"We would move forward except for the winter weather."

Regarding the motivational dynamic of these word patterns, if you tell buyers who frequently use possibility-driven words that they *have to*, *should*, or *must* take an action, they will emotionally push back. They don't *have* to do anything. They *choose* what they want to do. Bottom line? The more frequently buyers use possibility-driven words, the more your presentation needs to address what the buyers can do and what they want to do.

If you tell buyers who frequently use necessity-driven words what they can do or what they want to do, there is a good chance they will do nothing. They are motivated by what they *must* and *have to* do. Often they do not take action until they believe they are forced to take action.

The idea of using necessity-driven words to motivate buyers goes against the positive atmosphere many salespeople work to maintain. However, as sales professionals, part of the service that we provide to buyers includes presenting our products in a manner that makes sense to the buyers. *We* may not buy products that way, but our presentations are not about our decision-making processes. Design everything in your presentation to help the buyers say yes.

3. Feeling, hearing, seeing

At any given moment during a sales presentation, the buyer is experiencing feelings, having an internal conversation, and making mental images about what you are saying. While all three types of thought occur simultaneously, most buyers tend to pay attention to one type of thought more than the other two. How do we know which type of thinking a buyer is paying attention to? One indication is the type of words he uses most frequently.

For example:

a) Feeling words

Some buyers frequently use words that express feelings. Feeling words include touching words and temperature words.

"I don't *feel* that is a good idea."
"I am trying to *get a handle* on our finances."
"We haven't *grasped* that concept."
"We think it is a *hot* idea."
"It's *hard* for me to understand."

b) Hearing words

Some buyers frequently use words that express how they talk to themselves about your product and services. Hearing words include descriptions of sound.

"That *sounds* good to me."
"I *hear* what you are saying."
"Let's *harmonize* our thoughts about this."
"Our organization is experiencing *discord* on this topic."
"That name *rings* a bell."

c) Seeing words

Some buyers frequently use words that express the images in their minds about your products and services.

"*See* what I mean?"
"I get the *picture.*"
"We have a *bright* future…"
"*Focus* on this concept…"
"She has a *colorful* personality."

122

Do people often mix feeling, hearing, and seeing words? Yes. Some words are spoken by habit. Is this an exact science? No. We do not need to clinically analyze buyers to recognize their word patterns. Just notice the frequent behaviors of buyers, adjust your behavior appropriately, and move on.

Note: Always be cautious of putting buyers in boxes. There are no "feeling" people or "hearing" people.

The purpose of noticing which type of words buyers use frequently is to use those same types of words during your presentations. Imagine a salesperson asking, "Do you get the big picture? Are you seeing the benefit?" The potential client answers, "We don't feel this is in our best interest. We are cool to the idea of taking action right now." The mismatch in language can lead a buyer to believe that she is not connecting with you. It won't necessarily be a conscious awareness for her. It's more likely to be an unconscious recognition that creates sales resistance.

A buyer's behavior can also indicate which mode of thinking he is paying the most attention to. A buyer who pays the most attention to his feelings generally:

- talks a bit slower;
- looks down as he is thinking; and
- makes decisions more slowly, because it takes him a while to figure out how he feels.

If you talk faster than the buyer does, his discomfort may disrupt your rapport. Slow down. Use feeling words, and if he looks down to think about what you are saying, briefly break your eye contact to allow him a few moments of private thought.

A buyer who pays more attention to her internal conversations tends to:

- speak in a more rhythmic manner and with a rich voice;
- look side to side when she is thinking or talking;
- make decisions more quickly than buyers who pay more attention to their feelings, but still think in analog (one word at a time); and
- notice if you do not articulate your words clearly or if your voice is thin or scratchy. Therefore, pay attention to your enunciation and use hearing words.

A buyer who pays most attention to the images in her mind tends to:

- speak most quickly (Why? Because each image is loaded with information. Remember the old saying about a picture being worth a thousand words?),
- look up when she is thinking of an image, and
- make decisions the quickest.

If you speak more slowly than the buyer does, the difference may disrupt your rapport. Speak faster. Use seeing words and get to the bottom line. Concisely say what you have to say, and ask for action. Time is not your friend when making presentations to buyers who pay most attention to the images in their minds.

The takeaway from word patterns is to look for the obvious indicators. The more your buyers use a word pattern, the more important it is for you to include those word patterns in your presentations. It would be a shame for you to present compelling solutions to a willing buyer who is emotionally distracted by the word patterns you use to describe your products and services. Discover the word patterns of your buyers and speak in a similar manner to how they think.

THE VISUAL PRESENTATION

When appropriate, allow your physiology to show what you are saying.

- If your words say you are excited about your product, then show that excitement in your facial expressions.
- If you are talking about something big or referring to a specific part of your brochure, use hand gestures to draw attention to the meaning of your words.

In general, remain aware of your physiology when you are making presentations.

- Is your facial expression pleasant?
- Are you smiling?
- Is your eye contact appropriate?
- Do your eyes reflect feelings of confidence or anxiety?
- Do your gestures indicate enthusiasm?
- Is your posture relaxed or tense?
- Do you habitually shake your head no as you speak?

How do you nonverbally respond when a buyer asks a tough question or says *no*?

- Does the smile drain from your face?
- Do your eyes avert to one side to avoid revealing that you are emotionally regrouping?
- Does your posture sag with disappointment or stiffen for battle?
- Does your facial expression show appreciation that the potential client has chosen to communicate the issues that must be addressed before he can say *yes*?

- Does your posture remain consistent throughout the presentation and indicate you are ready to hear the buyer's concerns?

You have few secrets from your buyers. During your presentations, make sure that your nonverbal behaviors communicate the same message as your words.

VISUAL AIDS

Using visual aids that clearly indicate what you are saying increases the retention of listeners. Examples include:

- illustrations
- samples
- product demonstrations
- videos

Even if you dislike the visual aids provided by your company, we encourage you to find some way of using or at least referencing them. Show illustrations that communicate emotion. From your company's literature, find several images that reinforce the emotion that you are communicating about your product. Gesture to those images as you cover features and benefits during your presentation. It will help reinforce the emotions you want to create in your buyers.

HUMOR—BE CAREFUL!

Always be careful with humor during a sales presentation. Whether used before, during, or after the presentation, humor can either warm or chill the hearts of your buyers. Humor can deepen your rapport or kill it. If you easily joke with people, humor can be an asset. If you are using humor because it is built into your company's presentation, rehearse your delivery until you can deliver it naturally.

Above all, avoid sarcastic humor, put-down humor, and political or religious humor. Do not joke with a buyer as you would with close friends. While you are encouraged to be authentic with buyers, your first priority is to remain professional at all times during the sales appointment.

Self-deprecating humor is usually a safe form of humor. People tend to like others who do not take themselves too seriously.

Note: Do not joke about your professional abilities. Buyers may interpret that type of humor as an indication of lack of confidence.

"Aw, I forgot my business cards again. I'm such an airhead."

"Oh, I'm so bad at math. Where would I be without a calculator?"

Playfully joking about yourself in nonbusiness matters can be endearing...when used sparingly. It communicates a strong level of self-confidence. You have the self-assurance to laugh at yourself in areas that others can relate to.

One last consideration about humor: just because your buyer tells a joke with dark humor does not mean you have permission to tell the same type of joke. Call it unfair, but a buyer may decide it is inappropriate for a salesperson to tell the same type of joke that she told just a few minutes earlier. When in doubt...don't!

Now let's examine the positive uses of humor. In addition to increasing your likability and deepening your rapport, humor encourages buyers to breathe. When buyers are listening intently or considering a buying decision, they sometimes unknowingly tense their bodies. Humor allows them to relax. That can extend their attention span during your presentation. The most persuasive use of humor is to use it to move the presentation forward. For example, if part of your presentation includes the idea that people commonly delay taking action to find a solution, you may tell a funny story about someone who procrastinated. In addition to relaxing the buyer and increasing your rapport, the humor can also move your presentation forward by introducing or illustrating the topic of procrastination.

Some salespeople give brief presentations of three minutes or less. Others have presentations that last fifteen minutes or more. The longer your presentation, the more frequently you should break it up with humor. Just always make sure that any joke you add into the mix is time-tested to be funny and not offensive in any way.

Where do you find effective humor? Bookstores have a variety of sources to choose from. Another source is listening to everyday humor with an ear for applying it to your presentation. Magazines, talk shows, and speakers at business or nonbusiness organizations all use humor. Don't just listen. Listen for something you can use during your sales appointments. Just make sure the humor fits your personality and your type of product.

USING FIRST NAMES

There are two extremes regarding the use of someone's name during the presentation. The first extreme is never using the buyer's name. The other is to use the buyer's name too frequently.

Some salespeople avoid using the names of their buyers because they are difficult to pronounce. As a rule, do your best to learn the proper pronunciation of every buyer's name. Then use your judgment about whether or not to attempt to pronounce the name a few times during your presentation. If people have unusual names, you can assume that they are used to helping others pronounce them. Showing an interest in getting it right demonstrates your desire to serve them well.

More often than not, the root cause for not using a buyer's name is that you've forgotten it! The busier you are and the more buyers you see each day, the easier it is to forget. Forgetting your buyer's name will diminish your confidence during the sales appointment, and it will show. Easy access to a written list of your appointments can serve as a backup when a buyer's name slips your mind.

To help you remember names, try repeating the names to yourself *at least four times* when you first hear them. Also, use the buyers' names as soon as it makes sense to do so in your presentation. Knowing that you plan to use them sometimes helps you to remember. And after you've said their names out loud in your presentation a couple of times, you won't be as likely to forget them.

The second extreme is constantly using a buyer's name during the presentation.

"Harold, you are correct in saying…"
"Harold, would you say that…?"
"As you know, Harold,…"
"Harold, how often have you…?"

A note of caution: If you overuse a person's name, the buyer may perceive it as a sales gimmick or an annoying habit. Either way, it will diminish the rapport you established earlier in the sales appointment and distract the buyer from your presentation.

THE HEART OF PERSUASION

The last three topics are the very heart of persuasion during your presentations.

1. Selling with benefits

The concept of selling the benefits of each feature is one of the most foundational sales principles taught. And yet...*it is frequently only half-done by salespeople when they plan their presentations.* Features are presented. Benefits are not given their due. Why would one of the most frequently taught subjects in sales be one of the most neglected skills that are regularly practiced? There are several possible reasons why features dominate the thoughts of salespeople during their presentations and lead to the neglect of explaining the benefits.

- Features are usually tangible. The features are more easily recognized and discussed than the less tangible benefits. The company brochures and product demos discuss what the product is and show what the product does.
- Features are exciting and interesting! Even before you get to the benefits that motivate buyers to say *yes*, some features are pretty cool.
- Features *can* lead to assumptions. It is easy to assume that buyers will connect the dots and see the "obvious" benefit of the feature.

  The safety switch...protects workers.
  The twenty-four-hour service line...means better customer support.
  The titanium casing...means less weight but the same strength.

It's so obvious...to *you*. Do not assume it is equally obvious to buyers. Notice how that assumption compares in the progression of the examples below.

- *"This is the feature."*
- *"Now that I have described the feature, this is what it does...[spell out benefits]."*
- *"Now that I have described the feature and the benefits, how do you think this feature will benefit your business?"*

In the first example, the benefits of the feature are left undescribed under the assumption that buyers will understand what they are.

In the second example, the benefits of the feature are explained in a statement.

In the third example, after the features and benefits have been stated, an open-ended question is asked to encourage conversation. The question shifts the buyer from passive listener to participant, and it reinforces the impact of the benefits by asking the buyer to state how those benefits apply to his needs.

Note: *You* may already know how those benefits apply to the buyer's needs. When *the buyer* states how they apply, he is confirming that your product will resolve his challenge.

The point of those three examples is to show how inadequate the first example is in ensuring that the buyer truly understands the key points of your presentation.

- A feature describes what the product/service is and what it does. "This product is a protective case for widgets."
- A benefit is what that feature does for the buyer. "The widget case will protect your widget in a situation where it might be dropped."

The common mistake made by salespeople during presentations is to enthusiastically explain the features of their product and then neglect to show buyers how it benefits them. The salesperson explains four or more exciting features of the product. "It's a turbo-charged, lightning-quick widget with titanium casing and a molecular coating of reinforced guava plant."

The guava plant coating is obviously meant as a joke. Our point is that many salespeople will use a sentence loaded with features and industry jargon, and not explain how the lightning-quick widget will save time for the buyer. Or how the titanium case will protect the widget from damage when the valet drops it. Or how the molecular coating will protect the widget from moisture so the buyer can take it indoors or outdoors.

When discussing features and benefits:

a) Start with the buyer's needs, which may be expressed or unexpressed. It is challenging to offer a solution to a buyer who does not believe she has a need. Often, you must verbalize the challenge that your buyer has never verbalized to herself.

b) Explain the feature of your product/service: show the buyer what it is and what it does. If you use industry jargon, make sure you explain the jargon. Better yet, don't use industry jargon at all. Then you don't need to remember to explain it.

c) Clearly explain the benefits of those features: how they address the buyer's challenges or add value.

Take a few moments now to identify the three most persuasive features of your product/service. Write down the potential challenges they address. Then explain in a sentence or two what your product/service is and what it does. Finally, explain how the product/service's features address those challenges and benefit your clients.

Need:
Feature:
Benefit:

If you find it is a challenge remembering to include the benefit with the feature, lead with the benefit and then explain the feature.

"You will save time [benefit] because the [feature] does this..."
"Your life will be less stressful [benefit] because our [feature] is available to..."

Wouldn't it be wonderful to present the features and the benefits of your product and have the buyer say, "Just last week, we had a situation where the [benefit of your product] was exactly what we needed"?

Buyers are often hesitant to offer such obvious buying signals, but you can design questions to ask before the presentation begins that discover those types of situations. Start with the most persuasive benefits of your products and services. Then build your questions around those benefits. Below are several examples of benefits, followed by questions that encourage buyers to talk about any situations that benefit would have addressed.

Guaranteed delivery: "How do late deliveries affect your business?"

Current online service records: "How valuable is it to have immediate access to service records when you meet with the board?"

Twenty-four-hour, live, manned service line: "How does it affect your business when clients call for service and hear a recording that the office is closed until the next business day?"

Flexible financing: "How does cash flow affect your ability to make the purchases you need to maximize your profits during the busy season?"

As you create and add these open-ended specialty questions to the other discovery questions you ask before the presentation begins, you are increasing the probability that the buyer will open up and tell you about his specific challenges. That knowledge will help you craft a relevant presentation and a compelling close.

Naturally, you will become excited about sharing the solutions your company offers to address those challenges. Consequently, the challenge for you will be to not begin selling right away. "Wowie-zowie! Have we got a product for you that would have saved you weeks of headaches! First, our product will…"

Hang on. Remember the three basic choices you have at any time during the sales presentation: (1) make a statement, (2) ask a question, or (3) remain silent.

The buyer just handed you a gift to help you close the sale. At that moment, while he is still open to talking about that challenging situation, ask one or two follow-up questions. Each additional bit of information you learn about his challenges will help you make more persuasive presentations and close sales more easily.

2. Selling value

Continuing the discussion about features and benefits, one specific application is selling value-based products and services against a price-based competitor. We mentioned this idea in chapter 8 with the discovery question "Is price your only consideration or is quality also important?"

In most cases, value selling is done during the presentation. Value selling part one goes something like this: "Our product is a greater value than our competitor's because of value A and value B." At the close, an average salesperson says, "Our price is [dollar amount]. Would you like to buy?"

The potential client, who rarely makes the connection between values A and B and the higher price of the product offered at the close, asks, "Why is the price so high?"

Then, value selling part two begins: "Remember when I talked during the presentation about how value A and value B will actually make our product more economical over the next twenty years than if you bought a cheaper product?"

At this point, the buyer often takes issue with the salesperson's claim about value A and value B and says, "Yes, but...I still think it is expensive." Now the conversation shifts to the merits of those two features. The salesperson repeats the same thing. "No, it is not expensive if you think about the next twenty years. You will save lots of money." The buyer says, "I'm not sure about the next twenty years, but I do know that at the next board meeting I will have trouble meeting this year's budget. This is just too expensive." The salesperson makes some more statements, and on it goes.

To remedy this situation, let's step back earlier in the sales appointment and find agreement on the bigger question of price versus value. When identifying needs, you ask the discovery question about price: "Is price your only consideration, or is quality also important?" With this question, you can come to an agreement with the buyer about the importance of quality long before you explain value A and value B.

When selling a value-based product, do you want to wait until the buyer raises the question of price during your presentation, or do you want to broach the subject proactively on your terms, when you wish?

- The former choice is wait-and-see selling. You wait until the presentation begins and hope that your presentation will persuade the buyer that your product is worth the higher amount.
- The latter choice is structured selling. Using the Circle of Persuasion, structure the sales appointment so you choose the moment and the method to most persuasively address the "value versus price" question.

Use the price discovery question to find agreement on the parameters of the "value versus price" question before you begin your presentation. When you lead the buyer to ask herself the right questions *before* the presentation begins, the right answers are more likely to follow during and after the presentation.

3. Heart-to-heart sales talks

There are times when everything has been said about a matter and the buyer is still undecided. At that point, a few words spoken from your heart—with complete sincerity—can assure the buyer of your intention to serve his needs well. You are stepping outside the role of salesperson for a moment and are talking to him as one human being to another.

Heart-to-heart talks involve statements of conviction. They are defined by *how* you express your thoughts as much as by what you say.

Heart-to-heart talks should be used sparingly. They are emotionally concentrated—a little bit goes a long way. You don't need to confirm if the buyer took to heart what you said. If you see by his nonverbal language that he was listening, then he got it. Say it and move on to the next topic in your presentation.

Note: If your work as a salesperson is simply a job you do to make money, then heart-to-heart talks are best left alone. Better to remain authentic than say something you don't believe just to get a sale. Remember, you have few secrets from your buyers. They can tell when salespeople don't really believe what they are saying.

Below are some examples to give you an idea.

Discussing value and higher price: "Jim, I realize we are not the lowest price in town. It is important that you understand why we never want to be the lowest price. When you are the lowest price, you may have to adjust the quality of your service to fit the price. My company doesn't do that. We are focused on doing what it takes to do the job right the first time."

If you say something such as that in a bland voice…it is just words. But when you look the buyer in the eye, lean forward a bit, and speak from your heart, then it becomes a heart-to-heart talk.

Heart-to-heart talks can also address challenges: "Sue, I'm not going to try to explain away the service you received. It was not what you paid for. My job is to make it right. We value your business, and this is how we are going to give you the service you deserve…"

You are not defensive. You are not ashamed. Great companies are not perfect companies. Great companies provide good value and quickly make things right when they don't fulfill customer expectations. Great salespeople address challenges quickly and use those unfortunate events to demonstrate the exceptional service they provide to buyers.

Heart-to-heart talks can be used at the close: "John, I realize you have choices. In our time together, you've heard me explain why I believe we are the best choice to deliver great service to you." (Summarize the benefits.) "The final reason is that when you do business with my company, you get me. It is important to me that you get great service. And I will be your inside advocate to make sure you get the best service we can possibly deliver."

The best part, of course, is that you really do care and you really are committed to giving great service.

Finally, regularly examine your presentation. Does every part of your presentation, in some manner, lead buyers to take immediate action? Your presentation is probably full of interesting facts and entertaining stories. Always remain mindful that each part of your presentation will move buyers either nearer to closing the sale or farther from it.

CHAPTER 9 KEY POINTS

- Every client contact provides an opportunity to give a presentation.
- When making presentations, your nonverbal behaviors continue to speak louder than your words.
- Whenever appropriate during your presentations, ask questions instead of making statements, because participating listeners are buying listeners.
- Learn to recognize word patterns in buyers and use those same patterns during the presentation: *want/avoid*; *can/must*; feeling, hearing, and seeing words.
- Visually show what you are saying with your gestures, with facial expressions, and with visual aids.
- Follow every mention of a feature with the benefit it provides.

10. Asking Closing Questions

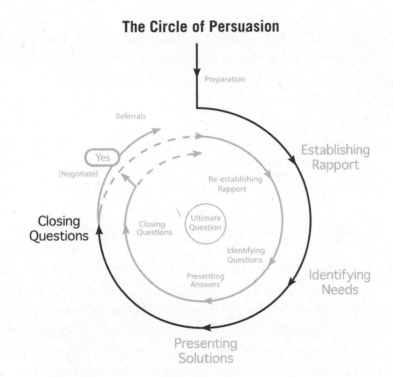

The Circle of Persuasion

Preparation

Referrals

Establishing
Rapport

Yes

(Negotiate)

Re-establishing
Rapport

Closing
Questions

Closing
Questions

Ultimate
Question

Identifying
Questions

Identifying
Needs

Presenting
Answers

Presenting
Solutions

Everything you've done to this point in the sales appointment is preparation to ask the buyer for the sale. Asking closing questions is what creates sales. That means asking directly and clearly for what you want the buyer to do. *If you want the sale, you have to ask.*

Thus far, you have taken the following steps around the Circle of Persuasion:

- You have established rapport, because buyers prefer buying from likable salespeople.
- You have asked discovery questions to identify the buyer's specific needs.
- You have presented solutions that addressed the buyer's specific needs.

Now you will ask the buyer to take real action, and you will guide her through the decision-making process. It's critical that you transition into asking closing questions smoothly, so as not to generate any discomfort or fear on the buyer's part (aka sales resistance). This transition can be a very frightening thing, especially for new salespeople. However, once this step is mastered you graduate from salesperson to sales professional, and your level of income follows.

WHAT IS THE BIG DEAL ABOUT CLOSING?

As mentioned earlier in this book, a lot of time and attention in training sessions goes to the presentation step of the sales process. This assumes the presentation will generate sales. When more time and attention are given to the many ways of asking closing questions—questions that call for buying decisions and action on the part of the buyer—that's when sales revenues really increase. Even though the point of asking closing questions is the climax of the sales process, it is the step that is most feared by salespeople.

Why do many salespeople fear asking potential clients to take action? Below are several reasons.

1. They fear being turned down or rejected

If you haven't learned this already, learn it now: you won't win every sale! When you've done your best and a qualified buyer doesn't buy from you, in most cases it's nothing personal. Do not consider a no-sale situation as a personal rejection.

2. They fear asking potential clients for their money

As youngsters many of us are taught that it's impolite to ask for anything—especially money. In selling, it's critical to remember that you're providing something in exchange for the buyer's commitment to own your product. You're not taking from them. The sales process is an exchange.

3. They fear asking at the wrong time and looking foolish

Some salespeople are uncertain when to ask for the sale. They look at the close as an isolated event, which makes the timing of the close even more puzzling. Sales pros continue their presentations until they believe their buyers have enough information to make a decision. Then they ask test or trial close questions to determine if the buyer feels ready to make a decision—all before attempting a final close.

4. They fear silence

Some salespeople are uncomfortable with silence. They just keep on talking. It's possible that they end up talking the buyer right out of the sale. *One of the most important lessons salespeople need to learn is that once they ask a closing question they should stop talking.* The buyer needs a moment of silence to think when making a decision. It is difficult for him to think while you are still talking. So be quiet.

5. They fear finding out they were wrong

Some salespeople fear they have wasted their time and effort in giving the presentation. They fear that they may have been wrong in determining that these buyers were well qualified and that their product was a great answer to the buyer's challenges. In some selling situations, you won't find out until after you've gone through the entire sales process that the buyer can't make a buying decision for a sound reason. Even top sales producers can tell stories of unusual circumstances they simply could not overcome.

Ironic, isn't it, that there is so much potential for fear on the salesperson's side of the selling process? Usually when we think about fear in selling situations, it's the myriad of buyers' fears that come to mind. At this point in the sales process, you are so close to achieving your goal of a closed transaction that you should feel excitement, not fear. It's the time to focus on every detail of the matter at hand—asking your closing questions.

If you learn one thing from this book: *The main show of the selling process begins at the close*, which is when most of the decision-making process occurs. Yes, some potential clients have already decided to buy when you get to the close. That's fantastic! And rare.

More often than not, when you attempt to close, a potential client will present questions, concerns, or negotiation requests. Guiding the buyer through those responses is where your skills as a sales professional shine. It's when anything can happen and when top professionals are ready to respond to everything that does happen.

By the way, the assumption of wait-and-see selling is that decision making occurs *during* the presentation. Most of the time buying decisions are made *after* the presentation. That is why the close is the main show. A salesperson's actions during the close are what separate the top sales producers from the rest of the sales team.

> Note: Many salespeople are involved in sales that require layers of approvals and, consequently, multiple sales calls. In this scenario, closing the sale on the first visit is not possible. In our definition, "closing the sale" means moving the sale forward by taking action on the next step. Every sales appointment has an action objective, even if it is to confirm the next meeting.

When the time to ask for a decision has arrived, the salesperson should summarize the points already presented and received favorably by the buyer, while covering both the advantages and disadvantages of the various actions offered. Such a benefit summary will help your buyer crystallize her thinking. You can never assume she will remember all the information you have shared with her and then make a buying decision. That's *your* job!

THE DIRECT CLOSE VS. THE TRIAL CLOSE

One of the most useful distinctions when closing the sale is the difference between a *direct close* question and a *trial close* question. A *direct close question* straightforwardly asks the buyer to take action.

"What purchase order number will be assigned to this, Sally?"
"How would you like to handle the investment for your order, Glen?"

A *trial close* question tests whether or not the buyer is ready to take action. It allows you to test the level of interest the buyer has in going ahead.

"If you were to approve the work order, what time of year would your tenants prefer us to begin the work?"

"If you were to refurbish your counters, would you want a wood or a mica finish?"

"If we became your service provider, would you want to take advantage of the annual billing discount?"

Buyers feel free to answer your trial close questions because their answers don't commit them to buying. In that sense, trial close questions are theoretical questions. You are merely asking buyers for information. In many cases, that information involves their opinion, and buyers love to give opinions.

The advantages of trial close questions are:

1. *The buyer remains relaxed.* The buyer does not feel the pressure of having to make a final decision. When he responds in the affirmative, he is giving you the same information that you would receive after he purchased your products or services. When he responds negatively or raises a concern about what you've asked, you've lost nothing and gained direction as to what else you need to cover before asking a final closing question.

2. *You can ask several trial close questions.* Long before you ask the buyer to take action, you can ask several trial close questions and gain information about virtually every aspect of his buying decision. Trial close questions give you valuable clues about where your buyer is in the decision-making process.

3. *You can ask trial close questions throughout the sales appointment.* One of the greatest advantages of trial close questions is that you do not have to wait until the close to get an indication of your buyer's willingness to make a positive decision. In

fact, you can ask trial close questions while you are identifying the buyer's needs.

PHRASING YOUR TRIAL CLOSE QUESTIONS

Trial close questions are a way of gauging just how warm or cold your buyers are about owning the benefits of your product or service. In many cases, they will begin with phrases like:

"If you were to go ahead..."
"If you were to move forward today..."
"If you were to take the next step today..."

The conditional word *if* makes the question theoretical and relaxes your buyer. With the first few trial close questions, these initial phrases will let your buyer know she can give you buying information without committing herself to taking action. When you ask many trial close questions throughout the sales appointment, it may become tiresome for your buyer to hear these introductory phrases each time you ask.

> Note: Redundancy indicates sales technique. You don't want your buyer to start wondering if you're trying to pressure or trick her into making a purchase. You want her to stay focused on the sales presentation.

After the first several trial close questions, leave off the introductory phrase (given in the parentheses below):

"Our products come in three colors. (If you decided to buy our product) How important would the choice of color be for you?"

"We have twenty-four-hour delivery. (If you were to order our products) Are there certain days you prefer to receive shipping?"

Trial close questions can help you gauge how close buyers are to taking action in two ways. First, if buyers are nowhere near taking action, they will tell you that instead of answering your question.

Salesperson: *"So, if the board approves the purchase, how soon would you want delivery?"*
Buyer: *"Whoa, we're not even ready to discuss this with the board yet!"*

In that example, the buyer didn't answer the question, but she did provide valuable information about how far the board is from making a decision.

If the buyer pushes back on your trial close questions, explain the purpose of your questions. "The reason I am asking is that summer is our slow season, and we can offer more flexibility in scheduling during those months." Ah, now they see that you are considering ways to benefit them, and they will be more inclined to answer future questions.

Other examples of trial close questions are:

"John, do you see why we are so excited about what this program is doing for our clients?"
"Mary, how are you feeling about what we've covered so far?"

With those questions, you are requesting feedback in order to determine the next step to take. If the feedback is positive, you're probably ready to ask your closing question. If it's negative, you will have at least heard a concern or been given something to work with as you step back into the presenting-solutions phase of the Circle of Persuasion.

After you receive a positive response to your trial close question, move smoothly into your final closing question with a proven closing strategy. One such strategy is the *Colin Powell Close*. It goes like this:

> John, former US Secretary of State Colin Powell has reportedly said, "Indecision has cost Americans, American business, and the American government billions more than a wrong decision." What we are talking about now is a decision, isn't it? What will happen if you say yes, and what will happen if you say no?
>
> If you say no, nothing will happen and things will be the same tomorrow as they are today. You'll face the same challenges that caused you to meet with me today.
>
> However, if you say yes, you can start enjoying all the benefits of ownership that we've been discussing.

Then list the benefits your buyer has agreed would be great for her company or her family. As soon as the list is complete, turn your paperwork around to the buyer. Hand her your pen, sit still, and be quiet! *Wait for her decision.* She will make one—either to own or not to own.

THE ORDER FORM CLOSE

When used with finesse, this close can be subtle and natural. Unfortunately, this close is often used too abruptly by salespeople who wait until the end of their presentation to pull out a sales form and start filling it out. The buyer may feel that you skipped a few steps and you are making assumptions without basis. Let's examine this situation more closely.

The best place to begin is with the reminder that it is always a good idea to have an order form with you. Even if you do not expect a decision from your buyer that day, include an order form among your other sales materials or visual aids.

Slightly spread out your visual aids so the order form can be partially seen. Let it silently create curiosity about the terms written on it. Let it silently imply it may be needed. Make it the little elephant in the room. Or, you might place it under a few sheets of your notepad. As you make notes during your conversation, you can note the information that would go on the order form by lifting just a few pages.

If your buyer asks what you're doing, simply say, "I have found that when I take good notes during conversations, I do a better job of remembering important details—especially details that might save my clients money or time. I jot down those important details on the paperwork so they won't be forgotten." See what you've done? You've just made filling out your form in the buyer's best interest. You'll be amazed at how well this works to your advantage.

If the buyer says he's not ready to sign any paperwork, simply say, "I understand. Believe me, that's the last thing I'm going to ask you to do." You may laugh as you read that last sentence, but please don't laugh when you say it to a potential client. Speak it with sincerity, and he'll relax. It's the truth. The last thing you ask for in most sales processes is the approval of the paperwork...but not now.

Next, stop calling the document or website page where you place your orders a "contract." We've discussed the importance of creating positive, powerful images in the minds of your clients with the words you use. What comes to your mind when you hear the word *contract*? It's a legal document. It's a commitment. It's likely you might have to go to court to get out of one. Replace the word *contract* with *agreement*, *paperwork*, or *form*, and watch how your buyer reacts. He won't jump on the defensive as he did in the past.

Another time to smoothly show your order form is when your buyer asks about your company's warranty. Pull out the paperwork to show that your company offers a warranty in writing. It is also natural to show your buyer where the order form specifies terms of payment, form of delivery, or any other details that will be important in the buyer's decision-making process.

After you show your buyer the relevant portion of the written agreement, lay it to one side.

Note: Do not place the order form too close to the buyer. Remember the proximity rule covered earlier about crowding people? The same is true about the proximity of an order form. Be gentle when physically moving a written agreement toward the buyer, so he doesn't think you are being too pushy. Better to set the order form a bit too far away from the buyer than too close.

When a buyer picks up the order form and looks at it, would you say that is a buying signal? When a buyer picks up *any* visual aid, that is a positive sign of interest! It does not mean he will buy, but it shows he is exhibiting curiosity about what you are saying. At the least, he is participating in the presentation, and a participating buyer has a greater tendency to make positive decisions.

So the order form is on the table throughout the presentation. Your buyer is giving you buying signals by asking questions about financing, delivery, styles, and so on. He nods in agreement with what you're saying. He looks through the visual aids.

The order form close is a one-two punch: using trial close questions to inch the buyer closer to taking action, and using the order form to show where you will record their answers.

"When would be the best time for delivery?"

"Do you track purchases with purchase orders or checks?"

"Would we deliver to your office or your warehouse?"

"Is the billing address at the local office or the home office?"

As the buyer answers these questions, use your order form as a visual aid, pointing to the section of the order form where that information will be filled in for financing, delivery, or model specifications.

You may or may not actually write in the information immediately. You will have to decide how positive his buying signals are before you take pen to paper or enter information on your computer. The value of referring to the order form is that you are helping your buyer become increasingly comfortable with the written agreement that formalizes his commitment to take action. When he does decide to move forward, filling out the written agreement will seem like a small step, because he is already familiar with it.

If your buyer is relaxed and positive, then when you confirm the billing address, fill in the address on your form. If the buyer does not stop you, continue filling out the rest of the form as the information you require is provided.

Note: Don't expect your buyer to provide the information you need in the same sequence that is on your order form.

Know your form so well that you can skip around it quickly and easily to add information. *Remember: selling is about making the buyer comfortable—not about making him conform to your needs.*

Set the filled-out form in front of the buyer and do a quick review. Point to each part of the form as you quickly review it. "We will deliver to this address. The billing is sent here. The financing method is _____." Set your pen down on top of the order form and point to where he will approve it. "Your signature goes here."

Notice the wording on that last sentence. You did not tell him to *sign* the agreement. When using this close, be wary of telling people what to do. Point out where their signature goes. Then sit back and look down at the order form.

You're relaxed and have a pleasant expression on your face. If you are feeling particularly persuasive, nod very slowly. By looking at the order form, you imply that their attention should be on the order form as well. Keep looking at the form until the buyer either authorizes it or expresses a question or concern.

If he asks more questions, whenever possible end the answer to each question by pointing to the appropriate section in the order form. For example:

Buyer: *"Can I pay for this with a credit card?"*
Salesperson: *"Is that the method you prefer to use? If so, we'll put the information here."* (Pointing to the area of the order form)
Buyer: *"Can I change the delivery date to next week?"*
Salesperson: *"Is next week the best time for you to take delivery? If that's the case, that information goes here."* (Pointing to the delivery date on the order form)

That is the order form close. Do you see how the methodology described above differs from the simplified version of concluding your presentation: pulling out an order form for the first time, and asking your buyer to confirm his address? By using the order form as a visual aid throughout the presentation, you make it familiar and nonthreatening during the close.

OTHER TYPES OF CLOSES

There are hundreds of ways to call for a decision. There is not room in this book to cover more than a few, though other resources for closing strategies are highly recommended, such as *How to*

Master the Art of Selling (Grand Central Publishing) and *Selling in Tough Times* (Business Plus), both by Tom Hopkins.

A popular and simple-to-use closing question is the *alternate advance close*. This close offers two choices to buyers. Instead of offering the buyer a chance to provide a *yes* or *no* answer, both of the choices you will give lead to a closed sale.

For example:

"Which do you think is a better solution for you: Product A or Product B?"

"Would you prefer to take delivery on Tuesday, or would Friday be better?"

"Shall we order these for you in Midnight Blue, or would you prefer Azure Breeze?"

This close is especially effective with people who do not want to be told what to do or have no idea what they want to do.

Another closing strategy to use is the *Ben Franklin close*, which visually appeals to buyers who are not responding to your auditory communication. This close is useful for buyers who are procrastinating. In fact, your buyer might say something like "I'd just like to sleep on this," or, "Let me weigh the facts and get back to you." Wise old Benjamin Franklin used and recommended making a list of the pros and cons of any decision. His process has been carried forward for hundreds of years because it is so practical and helpful.

So, when a buyer suggests putting off making a decision, you would say, "John, history has proven that most great decision makers believed a good decision was only as good as the facts. The last thing I would want to do is to influence you to make an unwise decision. However, if it proves to be a good decision, you would want to make it, wouldn't you?"

Not many people will avoid making good decisions.

"Fine. Let me help you. Let's draw a line down the middle of this paper. On this side, we'll list the reasons favoring the right decision today. Then, over here, we'll list the reasons against the decision. When we are through, we'll count up the columns, and you will be able to make the right decision. Let's see..."

You now list all the reasons for going ahead. Shoot for a minimum of six reasons. Then you warmly say, "Now, let's see the reasons you feel are against the decision."

You now sit quietly and let the potential client work on that side alone. After he is finished, say, "Well, let's see what we've got."

Add up each column—just the number of reasons; do not deliberate over whether some reasons carry more weight than others. Then say, "The answer is rather obvious, isn't it?" And you turn back to complete your paperwork.

A reminder: When wording your closing questions, use words that create pictures of what you want to happen. Avoid using words that create pictures of what you do not want to happen. If you say it, your buyer must briefly process that image in order to make sense of your words.

Words like *hesitation*, *delay*, or *cost* present images of negative actions you do not want your buyers to take. Terms like *act today*, *take the next step*, *participation*, and *fill out the paperwork* present images of actions you want your buyer to take.

Notice the difference in the examples below:

Negative: "What is your hesitation in making this decision?"
Positive: "What needs to happen for you to take the next step today?"
Negative: "Are you thinking it's too expensive?"
Positive: "What are your thoughts about the value of the benefits to your company?"

WRITE OUT YOUR CLOSE IN ADVANCE

The close can be a dynamic time in the sales appointment. Many salespeople wing their closing call to action, spontaneously creating the wording of their close as they say it. Some salespeople are good at spontaneous conversation, but the truth is, most are not. Most salespeople get through the close, but their call to action is filled with *uh*s and hesitations that water down the compelling nature of their close.

The momentary hesitations you have while you word your closing call to action are similar to the hesitations salespeople exhibit when they lack real conviction about their product. Might your buyer think that your uncertainty is about choosing your words, not your conviction about your product? No. All your buyer experiences is the subtle, nonverbal cues of uncertainty, and she notices those cues as you are asking her to take action. Internally, that wall of sales resistance will start to build again.

Do not leave the assumptions of your buyer to chance. When you ask your buyer to take action, there can be no hesitation for any reason, no uncertainty about the value of your product or service, no uncertainty about how you word your call to action.

How do you avoid uncertainty at the close? *Word for word, write down the final two or three sentences you intend to say to ask your buyer to take action.* Just the last few sentences. Then practice reading aloud what you have written until you can say it with confidence and the expectation that your buyer will take immediate action.

You will not read this in front of the buyer at the close, of course. You do not need to memorize it and recite it to your buyer. The purpose of practicing your close out loud is to create an easy path to follow so that at the moment of decision, a concisely worded close will be confidently spoken with a tone that assumes the buyer will naturally take the next step.

PUTTING YOUR KNOWLEDGE TO WORK

It is not enough to learn about closing the sale. You are not paid solely for what you know, but also for how effectively you apply what you know. Now that you have learned about closing the sale, put your knowledge to work. In the exercises below, write out a direct close, a trial close, and an alternate advance close for your product.

Here is a sample for selling widgets.

Product or Service: Widgets

Direct closes

"How many widgets would you like to order today?"
"What delivery date for this order is best for you?"

Trial closes

"If you were to order our widgets today, how many would you need immediately?"
"If you were to purchase our widgets, what size would you want?"

Alternate Advance closes

"Would you like to handle the investment by check or charge?"
"Did you want this shipped overnight or by regular ground shipping?"
"Did you want the extra year of support or the standard ninety days of support?"

Now it is your turn. Write out examples of these three types of closes. You may find it helpful to say your closes out loud to adjust the wording to how you naturally speak.

Your product or service:

Direct closes

a)
b)
c)

Trial closes

a)
b)
c)

Alternate Advance closes

a)
b)
c)

Then, prepare to use the Ben Franklin closing strategy. Take a piece of paper, draw a line down the middle of it, and list as many reasons for owning your product as you can possibly come up with. The more prepared you are before your sales appointment, the more likely you are to turn potential clients into happy clients.

THE TWO KEYS TO EFFECTIVE CLOSING

Whether you are just beginning your sales career or you are a veteran, beware of two common mistakes when closing the sale. They are simple yet costly mistakes that can undo all the persuasive selling you have done to this point. Even if your close was awkward or ill-timed, effectively implementing these two steps will move the buyer forward in the sale.

1. Remain relaxed

The first common mistake a salesperson can make during the close is to become tense. As mentioned earlier in the book, his physiology shifts from being relaxed and engaging to being edgy or sometimes pushy.

The close can be a time of anxiety for you, because you are about to get a clear indication of how close the buyer is to making a decision. It can also be a time of anxiety for the buyer, because she is making a decision about parting with her own or her company's money.

A relaxed buyer can more easily make buying decisions. To help your buyer remain relaxed, it is important that you stay relaxed during the close. Why? Because throughout the sale, you have maintained a solid rapport with your buyer. As a result, you have been trading behaviors. If you suddenly become tense at the close, your buyer will follow your behavior and become tense as well.

Imagine the irony of the buyer, whom you have almost persuaded to take immediate action, suddenly becoming tense and indecisive—not because of anything that you said, but because of your actions! You suddenly became tense during the close, and she interprets her sudden, uncomfortable feelings as an intuitive warning not to take action. So above all, you must remain relaxed throughout the close.

Right now, take in a slow, deep breath and pleasantly smile. As relaxed as you are right now reading this book, that is how relaxed you should be when closing a sale.

Anxiety in buyers is not always about the actions of the salesperson. Some buyers become anxious not because of the decision you are asking them to make but because almost any decision they make creates anxiety. Deciding what clothes to wear each morning or what food to pull out of the refrigerator at night creates tribulation for some people. While this is an internal issue for the buyer, you can help relax her by remaining relaxed yourself.

2. Remain quiet

The second common mistake a salesperson makes during the close is to keep talking after he has asked the buyer to take action. The buyer needs time to think about the decision you asked her to make. As long as you keep talking, she will not have a chance to process all the information you gave during your presentation. Remain quiet and give her a chance to consider her decision.

When you continue to talk through the close, this signals to the buyer that you are not finished giving her information.

Consider the flow of questions and statements throughout the sales appointment. When the sales appointment began, you asked questions about areas of common interest to establish rapport. Then you asked business-related questions to identify the buyer's needs. During the presentation, you made statements to provide the information to make a decision. Now, at the close, you have invited the buyer to take action by asking a question.

The buyer grows quiet as she thinks about buying. But before she is finished thinking, you begin selling again by making these kinds of statements:

"Remember, you get 10 percent off if you act by the end of the month."

"And the shipping is free if you order more than one hundred items."

"And the purchase includes one year of customer support."

Here's the challenge: the very structure of your communication will distract and confuse the buyer. Your closing question indicated it was time for the buyer to make a decision. Now your additional statements suggest you're not yet finished giving the buyer reasons to buy. That leads the buyer to unconsciously begin to wonder if she has enough information to make a decision.

A confused mind says…*no*. That ambiguity can create just enough confusion to delay a decision. Even worse, it can take a buyer who was ready to say *yes* back toward indecision. That is the importance of avoiding this mistake. Remaining quiet during the close helps you avoid losing sales that you already made during your presentation.

The format of effective closing is simple. At the end of your presentation, when you ask your buyer to take action, take a slow, deep breath and relax. Then remain quiet until your buyer responds to your closing question.

YES, NO, MAYBE

Once this simple format becomes second nature, you will begin to enjoy the moments of decision rather than fearing them. This is when anything can happen. Your buyer may exclaim, "Yes! I'll take two!" Or she may ask questions or express concerns. (Those are *maybe*s.) Or she may say, "Never! Not in a million years!" But your buyer will not sit there indefinitely and say nothing.

She will respond because of the demands on her time and because she has needs that require solutions. By this point in the sales appointment, her responses will rarely be absolute *no*s, because she would have likely said so earlier. Most of the time, she will say *yes*, ask a question, express a concern, or ask to negotiate the terms of the sale.

That brings us back to where we began this book: when the buyer says *no*. All the great sales professionals hear *no*. In fact, few buyers will say *yes* the first time you ask. So be ready mentally and emotionally for any variation of the three basic responses. In fact, anticipate the buyer's response. The main show has begun! This is when you will earn most of your money and distinguish yourself as a top sales professional.

Scenario 1: Business Sales Appointment

Kate believes her presentation is drawing near to the close.

While giving her presentation, Kate talked about what Mr. Stevens wants to happen—for his teams to finish their projects on schedule—rather than what he wants to avoid. She used words like *can, could,* and *want* to match the possibility words used by Mr. Stevens. She matched his feeling words like *get a handle, calm, feeling.* She slowed down and matched his rural pace of speaking. She also varied her style of presenting, using her tablet to show slides of various widget models and, when appropriate, gesturing to illustrate her words.

Most important, she tied every feature of her product and services to the benefits that would help his business. When she discussed features that added to the reliability of Widget Corp's widgets, she tied it back to how they could help him avoid repeating past situations that caused costly delays for his teams in the field.

Now Kate is ready to close. She begins by asking some trial close questions. "Dean, you mentioned that several of your widgets have been underperforming. If you were to replace your unreliable widgets, how many would you be getting?"

"The incidents we have had this past year involved two widgets, but a third widget is showing signs of extreme wear."

Kate isn't sure if he is indicating buying two widgets or three, but as a general rule she always rounds up to the next highest number. The purpose of her next trial close question is to determine which model she is going to ask him to buy. "Were you thinking about the standard model or the deluxe model?"

"Well, for our work, the deluxe model makes more sense. We place too much demand on our widgets during business hours to trust the capacity of the standard model."

"Dean, do you see why we are so excited about what our widgets are doing for our clients?"

"I do. The quality is definitely better than what we're using now. And if your service is as good as you say it is, I will give it serious consideration."

"Great! Shall we place your initial order for three widgets, or would you rather start with two?"

Mr. Stevens sits back in his chair and makes some mental calculations. He looks at the image on her tablet. He looks at some papers on his desk.

As he thinks, Kate patiently sits with an expectant, pleasant expression. She is not sure what he will do next, but she is satisfied with the selling points they discussed to bring him to this point of decision. She looks down at her tablet to give him a few moments of privacy as he thinks.

Finally Mr. Stevens speaks: "We're in the middle of our busy season right now. I'm not sure it is a good time to switch. I'm not getting reliable service now, but for the price it's been getting us by."

The closing moment passes as Mr. Stevens verbalizes a concern that is stopping him from taking immediate action. Their journey around the outer circle ends, and their journey around the inner circle is about to begin.

Scenario 2: Residential Sales Appointment

Bob's presentation is coming to an end. During the presentation, he uses *must* words to match Gary's and Pat's words, like *have to* and *need to*. He also uses hearing words like *sounds good, rings a bell,* and *harmonize.* Since Pat and Gary talk about what they want to avoid in the future, Bob talks about the actions they must take to avoid that unwanted scenario. Bob is not overly dramatic. He simply presents his product in the light of helping them avoid the bad future scenario they don't want rather than describing the positive scenario they do want. It is not Bob's nature to talk that way. He and his wife always talk in terms of what they want, not what they don't want. But he is selling to Pat and Gary and needs to speak their language.

Bob uses third-party news stories to address their concerns about the widget industry. He shows them consumer reports that rate Residential Widgets near the top of its industry. He uses a company brochure to show the features and benefits of Residential Widgets's product. His benefits are designed for situations that Pat and Gary have not yet experienced but are clearly concerned about. Bob keeps the written agreement directly underneath the company brochure. As he picks up and sets back down the company brochure during the presentation, Pat and Gary have a clear view of the Residential Widgets written agreement. When Pat asks about the length of Residential Widgets's customer support, which comes with the widget, Bob shows her what's written in the agreement. When Gary asks about the warranty, Bob shows them the section in the written agreement specifying the length of the warranty. As a result, by the end of the presentation, Pat and Gary are familiar with the sight of the written agreement.

Now Bob is ready to begin the close. He starts with several questions that elicit a *yes* answer. "You mentioned that Diane will finish college next year and she will probably be moving out of the house."

Pat and Gary nod in agreement.

"And we've discussed the benefits of the Residential Widget to your family and the advantages of taking action sooner rather than later." Bob briefly summarizes those benefits. Again, they both nod in agreement.

Bob picks up the written agreement and points to the warranty section. "We've discussed the warranty," he says to Gary. "And we discussed the customer support," he says to Pat. Bob turns the agreement around to face him and picks up his pen. "Now I assume that you would want the widget shipped here to the house?"

"We receive all of our shipments here at the house, but..." Pat looks at Gary.

Bob continues, "And are mornings or afternoons best to receive shipments?"

"Well...," Gary says with uncertainty.

Bob waits for Gary to answer. Bob did not ask a direct close question, but with the paperwork close, Bob's objective is to continue asking a series of trial close questions until Pat and Gary either complete the written agreement and say *yes* or they stop him from proceeding. Bob guesses that Gary has not revealed the reasons for his hesitation yet. These trial close questions are the best way to bring those reasons out into the open.

Gary is at the moment of decision. Bob senses that Gary is having an internal conversation about making a buying decision, and he gives him time to think. Gary finally continues, "We are not sure this is a good time."

Bob reflects back Gary's words with no emotion: "You're not sure if this is a good time?"

Pat cuts in, changing the subject. "I'm not sure I will understand how to benefit from the widget. I'm not very good at learning about these sorts of things. What if something happens to Gary?"

With Pat's question, the moment of decision passes. They have completed their journey around the outer Circle of Persuasion. Now they are beginning their journey around the inner circle.

CHAPTER 10 KEY POINTS

- If you want the sale, you have to ask for it.
- Understand and work with the fears on both sides of the selling situation.
- The main show of the sales process is not the presentation; it's the close.
- It's important to summarize the points already presented and received favorably by the buyer before attempting to call for a decision.
- Direct close questions should clearly ask the buyer to take action.
- Trial close questions gauge how close the buyer is to taking action.
- After asking a closing question, remaining relaxed is as important as remaining quiet.
- Do not interrupt the buyer's thinking process.

SECTION 3

—

When Buyers Say No

11. Re-establishing Rapport

The Circle of Persuasion

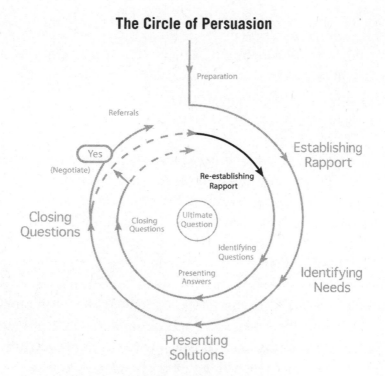

THE INNER CIRCLE

Congratulations! As illustrated above, you have now completed the *outer* circle of the Circle of Persuasion, and you have led your buyer to a decision point. You asked your buyer to take immediate action toward the purchase. The buyer said *no*. He may or may not have given you a reason why he said *no*—yet. But that's okay.

This is the point in the sales process where this book actually began. That's because it is the precise point that stops many salespeople from moving forward with a sale. When they hear *no*, they begin to implement their exit strategies and start thinking about their next meetings, about where they'll stop for a snack or coffee, or about the phone calls or e-mails they need to handle. In other words, as soon as they hear the word *no*, they start to mentally check out of the sales process.

You, however, understand that there is another path to pursue after hearing the buyer's first few *no*s. Even so, it's important to think about the *no* that you just received.

It's time for a quick reality check.

- Were you prepared for *any* response? Or did the buyer's negative response truly catch you off guard?
- Did you mistake the buyer's signals for a commitment to buy?
- Was there a concern you missed that is holding the buyer back?

When the buyer is smiling and participating, that's good, but don't get ahead of the game. You must always be prepared for a buyer to put the brakes on the sale at any point during the sales process. With positive buying signs, you are heading in the right direction, but **the sale is not closed until you receive both the authorization and the investment you need to complete the sale.**

What if the buyer is not smiling or participating? That is not as pleasant, but do not become prematurely negative and decide during your presentation that he won't own your product today.

- Maybe the buyer doesn't fully understand the benefits yet.

- Maybe he is giving serious thought to how your product will benefit him.
- Maybe he has developed a kind of "poker player" style of buying, where he takes pride in not giving buying signals during the presentation.

Whatever the reason for his behavior, as long as the buyer continues to listen, you still have a chance to close the sale. Remember to align your behavior with his. A cool buyer may suddenly warm up when you stumble upon a hot button of his. This is where paying attention to body language is so critical. In fact, nonverbal cues are often easier to recognize than verbal ones.

> Note: In remote selling, such as online or over the phone, you may notice an increase in the number of questions asked or a slight change in the buyer's tone of voice—expressing more interest than previously.

The silver lining to the dark cloud of a *no* is that any unexpected or unpleasant event during the sales appointment is an opportunity to demonstrate that you are a true sales professional. Some buyers, for reasons unknown, seem to enjoy trying to fluster salespeople. When you handle their questions, comments, and even unexpected actions with a professional calm, their level of confidence in you goes up. Expect the best and be ready for anything! When you are prepared, the worst they have to offer is never all that bad.

MAYBE MEANS *NO*, TOO

Bear in mind that instead of saying *no*, some buyers will say *maybe*. As covered at the beginning of this book, you must treat a *maybe* like a *no* simply because it's not a *yes*. A *yes* is when your buyer takes the actions of approving the paperwork and/or giving you money in exchange for your product. A *maybe* and a *no* are when your buyer does not approve the paperwork or give you money. It's that simple.

Because many sales careers have been shipwrecked on the rocks of *maybe*, consider that *no* and *maybe* are often the same answer given with different wording. Many buyers use *maybe* as a polite or nice way of saying *no*. Some salespeople delude themselves into thinking that any answer but a *no* is okay. So they hang on to the hope that if they keep talking long enough, buyers will eventually give in and say *yes*.

Do not allow yourself to be fooled into thinking that the *maybe* is a sale that has already occurred but is just not completed yet. If you do, you are misleading yourself. After all the time you spent arranging the sales appointment, all the effort you've given during the sales presentation to lead the buyer to an educated buying decision, the response could be that the buyer still wants to delay her decision. *Maybe*s are often signs of procrastinators.

To multiply your sales revenues, you will want to spend the majority of your time with buyers who are able to say *yes* now. The rest of this section is dedicated to the strategies to employ when buyers do not take action after you ask your initial closing question.

The Circle of Persuasion demonstrates how to keep the sales process moving forward after hearing those *no*s and *maybe*s. In fact, some *maybe*s will be stopping points in the sales process. But you will not know that until you complete the journey around the inner circle, which will be covered in the next few chapters. At the end of *that* journey, if you encounter *maybe*s that are stopping points, develop a plan for continuing to work with those buyers until they can give you a *yes*. Then decide how much and what type of effort you should put into working your list of *maybe* potential clients.

THE GREAT DISCOVERY

Remember the four steps of selling covered in chapter 4? (1) Establishing Rapport; (2) Identifying Needs; (3) Presenting Solutions; (4) Closing Questions.

At this point in the sales process, the Circle of Persuasion provides a surprising insight. When addressing a question or concern, you perform the *same four steps* that you followed to lead the buyers to the first decision point! After you hear the initial *no*, the move through the inner circle of the same steps goes much faster and brings you nearer to the close. This is a profound discovery for many salespeople.

The inner circle allows you to know *when* to ask questions, *when* to make statements, and *when* to remain silent. In short, it provides you with the tools to move buyers to another point of decision with the same confidence and competence that you've enjoyed up to this point in the sales process.

In contrast, instead of following this planned path back to a closed transaction, most wait-and-see salespeople either remain silent or play a game of question-and-answer ping-pong with buyers. During this verbal game, buyers tend to take control. They may have said *no* to the initial closing attempt, but they are still interested enough to ask questions. This is a buying sign that experienced sales professionals inwardly smile at as they move into the inner Circle of Persuasion.

Wait-and-see salespeople, however, answer every question and then remain silent, as if their answer was another close. This gives buyers complete control over what happens next in the sales process. At the very least, those wait-and-see salespeople would benefit from learning to provide answers to the buyer's questions and then follow with questions of their own in order to keep control of the conversation.

As an example, let's say a client asks if the product could be delivered by the fifteenth of the month. The typical salesperson will answer yes or no and then say nothing. A properly trained salesperson will turn the answer into a call-for-action question by asking, "Bob, if I can guarantee delivery no later than the fifteenth of the month, are you ready to go ahead and place your order today?" That question is another direct call to action. "If I can... will you?"

If the delivery date is the final detail keeping the buyer from making decisions, he'll answer in the affirmative, and you've just made the sale. If he hesitates, there are likely other details that need to be addressed before he feels he can commit. But now you know a bit more about his concerns.

When you don't know what's holding the buyer back, it's like trying to put your arms around a ghost. There's nothing solid for you to grab hold of. When you tie questions to your answers that keep steering the conversation toward a closed sale, you're turning those ghosts into something concrete to work with.

As with your journey around the outer circle, persuasion in the inner circle is like a game of chess. The early moves will determine the later responses from the buyer. And along the way, you will discover two differences in traveling around the inner circle versus the outer circle.

1. Each step in the inner circle happens more quickly than those in the outer circle.
2. When *re-establishing* rapport in the inner circle, you make statements rather than ask questions. More on that in the next section of this chapter as we examine the first step in addressing a question or concern.

RE-ESTABLISHING RAPPORT

The first step in addressing a question or concern after hearing the initial *no* is to re-establish rapport. Let's review what occurred to temporarily affect the rapport you enjoyed during the sales presentation.

1. You asked your buyer to make a decision

For many buyers, making *any* decision is an uncomfortable experience. As a result, the discomfort created by *asking* a buyer to make a decision can temporarily disrupt rapport, especially when the buyer is asked to make decisions involving her time or money. Money decisions are often emotionally charged, drama-filled events. Most people hate to part with their money. Most people also want to feel that they've made a good decision on behalf of the company or their family. This adds up to a lot of pressure.

2. You asked your buyer for money

Up to the point of asking for the sale, it's easy for the buyer to feel you're on her side.

- You are friendly.
- You are taking a sincere interest in her needs.
- You are educating her.
- You are being very helpful.

When you finally ask the buyer for money, the entire dynamic of your interaction with her can, and often does, change. Mentally and emotionally, the buyer sees you switch from being a helpful friend to being a determined opponent who has designs on her money. Her defenses—her resistance to the sale—have been raised. You have to overcome that feeling in your buyer by re-establishing rapport, in essence settling things down, before she'll allow you to take on the role of helpful advisor again.

3. Your buyer did not comply with your request

Another factor that temporarily affects rapport is when your buyer does not take action as you requested. In other circumstances, your buyer might be a people pleaser. People who enjoy pleasing others usually do not enjoy saying *no* to others.

Noncompliance is uncomfortable and can temporarily disrupt your level of rapport. In this case, the buyer may start to feel awkward in your presence—you're someone she's turned down. She may start wanting the sales process to end and hope you will leave. Your job is to assure her she did not cause you to stop wanting to help her or to dislike her just because she didn't go along with your initial request.

> Note: During the actual moment of decision, it is okay if your buyer is a little uncomfortable. She has to create and accept change in order to own the benefits of your product. And change is uncomfortable for most people.

Avoiding the pain of decision partially explains why the buyer will introduce a question or concern that may seem unrelated to your discussion, rather than coming right out and saying *no* to your closing question. By voicing a question or concern, she moves away from the moment of decision. That's okay as long as you know where you are in the sales process and what to do next. Buyers who do this are saying *maybe*. She is interested enough to keep the conversation going...as opposed to saying *no* and dismissing you.

But whatever the buyer's reasons are for not taking action quickly, start re-establishing rapport by letting her know it is okay that she did not go ahead. It's just as important to re-establish rapport as it was to establish it in the first place. With re-established rapport, the buyer will be more likely to trust the content of what you say as you respond to the questions and concerns that are holding her back. Remaining likable during the uncomfortable process of making a decision works in your favor, because buyers like to do business with likable salespeople.

As during the early part of the sales call, this is a penalty situation. Just because you remain likable does not mean the buyer will buy from you. But if you become *unlikable* during his decision-making process, he may prematurely end the sales appointment.

How do salespeople become unlikable after the close? They become tense. Their facial expressions reflect unhappy feelings of disappointment or impatience. Even worse, they become subtly belittling, implying with their nonverbal communication that anyone with common sense would have said *yes* by now.

The good news is that re-establishing rapport, like the other steps in the inner circle that will follow, takes just a fraction of the time it took to establish rapport in the outer circle. You can re-establish rapport with buyers with short statements such as:

"That's a great question. I'm glad you asked."
"I meant to cover that. Thank you for bringing that up."
"I understand your hesitation, Bob. Perhaps I misunderstood that aspect of your situation."

In just a sentence or two, you communicate that it is all right that your buyer didn't say *yes* right away. You re-established rapport that buys you extra time for leading the buyer back to a moment of decision. The buyer relaxes, and you move on to the next step of reviewing his needs to determine what might have been missed on the first go-around.

In review, when the buyer says *no*, always remain calm and

show him your confident, professional behavior. Then, work to re-establish rapport with short statements that let the buyer know it is okay that he didn't immediately say *yes*.

Make the buyer comfortable again. Work your way back to asking questions to make sure you understand more specifically what is keeping him from making a decision today.

CHAPTER 11 KEY POINTS

- As long as the buyer continues to be engaged, you have a chance to close the sale.
- Treat a *maybe* like a *no*, simply because it's not a *yes*.
- A buyer doesn't always say *no* because he lacks confidence in you or your product. It's often that he lacks confidence in his own abilities to make good decisions.
- Avoid playing games of question-and-answer ping-pong with the buyer after his initial *no*.
- The first step in addressing a question or concern after hearing the initial *no* is to re-establish rapport.

12. Identifying Questions

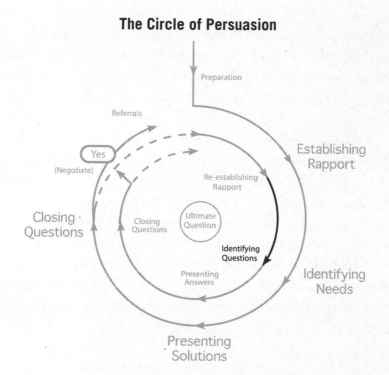

The Circle of Persuasion

Preparation

Referrals

Yes

(Negotiate)

Establishing
Rapport

Re-establishing
Rapport

Closing
Questions

Closing
Questions

Ultimate
Question

Identifying
Questions

Presenting
Answers

Identifying
Needs

Presenting
Solutions

Now that you have relaxed your buyer again by re-establishing a sense of rapport, the next step is to identify what the buyer is really saying—to get to the root of what is really holding her back. Then, you will create the optimal sales environment for presenting your answers to those questions or concerns.

In this next stop around the inner circle, you have two potential courses of action.

1. Do you choose to be *reactive*, waiting to see what questions and concerns the buyer raises next?
2. Or do you take a step back, look at your objectives for this part of the sales process, and be *proactive* about your actions to move the buyer forward toward the next moment of decision?

Before answering, take a moment to think about what your goal is for responding to the buyer's questions and concerns. Be aware that your answer will influence your actions and the buyer's responses.

Many salespeople have the goal of providing information to answer questions and concerns. The assumption is that if the buyer runs out of questions and concerns, then…she must be ready to buy. In your selling experience, is that what usually happens?

The more questions or concerns the buyer has, the farther away she moves from the next moment of decision. Each of her questions provides the potential of leading the conversation away from the persuasive selling points of your product. That's why a solid understanding of questioning strategies is so critical to sales success.

How do you reconcile the desire to be of service to your buyer by addressing her concerns with your desire to move her toward the next moment of decision? The solution is in having a clear purpose and strategy to accomplish the following:

1. Discover all the questions and concerns that stop the buyer from saying *yes*.
2. Find out if the buyer will take immediate action after you satisfactorily address those concerns.

The key to achieving those two valuable objectives comes down to this one truth. Just because a buyer asks questions or raises concerns...*you do not need to respond right away*! You can ask questions. You can encourage the buyer to continue talking. You can remain silent. Do not be in a hurry to jump in with answers to questions and concerns!

Another key to help you achieve your objectives is to consider your role in this part of the sales process. Do you see yourself as a salesperson anxious to get to the next opening in the conversation in order to sell? Or do you see yourself as a consultant helping the buyer sift through her thoughts and feelings to make educated buying decisions? As a consultant, you will put as much effort into discovering the source of her hesitation as you did earlier in the sale identifying her needs.

There are five steps required to achieve the objectives listed above. With these five steps you will prepare buyers for your response to their questions and concerns. These steps may occur very quickly.

STEP 1: LISTEN!

The first step in responding to a concern is listening with the intention of understanding. One of the first keys in effective communication is to use your ears and mouth in the proper proportion. We all have two ears and one mouth. **As sales professionals, we should listen twice as much as we speak.** To gain the most from what you are hearing, work hard to become an empathetic listener. That means you pay total attention to what the buyer is saying. You watch his body language as he speaks. You look for clues as to what is really most important to him. You want to understand what questions the buyer is really asking. In short, what are his specific concerns?

Unfortunately, some salespeople are better at talking than listening. Have you ever spoken with someone who did not seem to be listening to you? The buyer will feel the same when you pretend you are listening but your thoughts are truly elsewhere.

When discovering the needs of buyers earlier in this book, you learned how salespeople use their bodies to nonverbally communicate with eye contact, nods, and leaning toward or away from the buyers. You will utilize those strategies again at this point in the sales process. **In addition to using your physiology to show you are listening, don't interrupt your buyer!** Why would a perfectly sane salesperson be crazy enough to interrupt a buyer who is sharing his concerns about buying the company's products and services? Frequently salespeople are tempted to interrupt when a buyer begins making statements based on wrong assumptions, inaccurate facts, or a misunderstanding of the information in the presentation. Because salespeople hear the responses of buyers on a regular basis, they *assume* they know what a buyer is going to say. Do not succumb to this temptation. Interrupting buyers can alienate them, especially when they may already be on edge about making decisions in regard to spending money.

Another reason to let the buyer finish talking is to allow him to release some pent-up emotions. He has listened to your presentation, and now he is making a minipresentation in response. Give him a chance to express himself. He will feel better for getting *his* thoughts out in the open—especially if he believes you are listening to what he is saying. You will learn more about what is stopping him from taking immediate action.

Note: In some cases, when a buyer explains what's holding him back, he may answer his own concerns. He may realize that a certain point *was* covered, but that he forgot. Allow him this opportunity.

This is a win-win situation for you and the buyer, though listening to his concerns is not always a pleasant part of the sales process. But remember, you will have plenty of time to address his inaccurate perceptions. Your objective for this part of the sales process is persuasion. Educating the buyer is an important part of persuading him to take action, but if you allow education to become your only goal, you may win the battle in making your point and lose the war in persuading him to take immediate action.

Another strategy to employ at this point in the sales process is to ask reflective questions. As discussed in chapter 7, asking reflective questions will increase the amount of information the buyer gives you. The hesitation among salespeople at this point in the sales process is that the buyer is giving reasons for not taking action. Should you encourage that?

Use your judgment based on what the buyer is saying. If the buyer is giving you additional information about his concerns or voicing new questions, then allow him to talk. The more the buyer tells you about his questions and concerns, the more knowledge you will have to help his move back toward a moment of decision. By giving the buyer simple reflective listening cues, you can significantly increase the amount of information he will share about his reasons for hesitating to say *yes*.

"What do you mean by...?"

"Please tell me more."

In contrast, if the buyer starts saying the same things over and over, or brings up unrelated subjects that move the conversation farther away from the next moment of decision, ask questions that move the conversation back on track.

STEP 2: RESTATE THEIR QUESTIONS AND CONCERNS BEFORE ANSWERING

After listening, the next step in this part of the sales process is to confirm your understanding of what buyers said with a summary of their questions and concerns. **Buyers do not always say what they mean.** Not clearly, anyway. This is especially true when they are experiencing the emotions involved in making decisions.

As time becomes more precious toward the end of the sales appointment, it is to your advantage to make sure that you confirm what is stopping the buyer from taking immediate action. Otherwise, you may spend valuable time addressing concerns that the buyer does not have. Your buyer may begin to focus on your lack of understanding of his concerns rather than on the buying decision itself.

There are distinct advantages to restating the buyer's concerns.

1. It shows him you are listening.
2. It allows the buyer to hear his own words. Sometimes a person's ideas do not make as much sense to him when he hears others repeat the same idea.

"To make sure I understand your question, you are asking..."
"So your concern is that... Is that correct?"
Occasionally the buyer will listen to your brief summary and correct what you say. That is great news!

• First, he is participating with you in a discussion, and a participating potential client is more likely to become a buyer.
• Second, you gain a more accurate understanding about what is stopping your buyer from taking action.
• Third, you will help calm the buyer because he will realize you finally understand the nature of his concerns.

The most persuasive advantage of restating the buyer's concerns and questions is using words that minimize the negative emotions the buyer has expressed. The content of your summary conveys the same thought, but you use words that reduce his strong negative emotions and amp his enthusiasm to a higher level. This is parallel to an earlier concept we discussed: saying what you want the buyer to do, and not saying what you don't want the buyer to do. Only in this case, you are shaping *the buyer's* words with a tone more conducive to making a buying decision!

Buyer: *"I don't believe your product [state benefit]."*

Salesperson: *"You are not certain yet if my product [state benefit]."*

Buyer: *"I'm angry that government regulations force us to..."*

Salesperson: *"You're unhappy that government regulations require you to..."*

Buyer: *"This price is far too high."*

Salesperson: *"You are wondering if the value is worth the investment."*

How do you respond when the buyer gives you a barrage of multiple concerns at one time? Will you have to remember every concern that is mentioned and address each one? Probably not. When your buyer gives you half a dozen concerns at once, you may be hearing his stream of thought, rather than a list of critical factors that would stop him from taking action. Some of his concerns, after being verbalized, will slip from his memory. The list is a challenge for him to remember, too!

As you patiently listen to all of them, you will begin to get a sense for which concerns are more important than others. Perhaps he spoke about one concern more passionately than others. If you forget to address a concern that is important to the buyer, he will probably bring it up again. Concerns critical to his decision-making process don't simply go away. You can confirm which concerns you believe are most important by asking a question such as "You brought up several concerns; would you say the most important is...? Am I correct in understanding that?"

STEP 3: FIND AGREEMENT

Whenever possible, find an element of agreement with the buyer's concerns. For example, you can agree with the buyer's feelings without agreeing with the content of his concern. Let's say that the buyer is upset at a costly government regulation clause in the sales agreement that he thinks is a waste of money. Even though you may believe the government regulation is in the best interest of the general public, you can agree that extra expenses can be upsetting.

Note: Be careful of responding to the concerns of buyers with the phrase "I understand." This phrase can be comforting and useful in conversations when you actually do understand what the potential client is saying. Unfortunately, it is often said by salespeople out of habit, whether they understand the buyer or not. Sometimes salespeople stop listening when a buyer is half-finished, because they decide what they will say next. On those occasions, "I understand" is really condescending code for "Stop talking. I heard enough to know that whatever you are about to say is wrong. Let me talk and I'll straighten you out."

You have few secrets from your buyers. They will sense when you are not listening to them. Many buyers will feel disrespected, because you are not extending the same courtesy of listening to their concerns that they just extended to you during your presentation.

In contrast, when you agree with the buyer on some aspect of what he said, it shows you are listening, and it creates a pleasant atmosphere in which to find agreement in the other areas that are preventing him from taking immediate action. Remember, you have not begun to *address* his questions and concerns yet. That will happen a bit later. For now, you are setting the tone by listening to his concerns and validating his perspectives by finding some aspects of agreement.

"I agree that…" are three magic words to begin your response to a concern! Below are several examples.

Concern: "I don't think I need this product."
Agreement: "I agree that you should invest only in products that help your business."

(You did not agree that the buyer does not need the product.)

Concern: "Your service team gave me bad service."
Agreement: "We certainly agree that all valued clients deserve great service."

(You did not agree that your service team actually gave them bad service.)

Concern: "Your customer service rep was rude to me on the phone."
Agreement: "I can appreciate your concern. I agree that my company's personnel should act professionally at all times."

(You did not agree that your customer service rep was rude on the phone.)

Note: Every action you take during a sales appointment is a choice with consequences. If you choose to engage the buyer in a discussion about the factuality of their concern, you will no

---

longer be discussing the buying decision. You must decide on the importance of that discussion, but you may end up winning the battle and losing the war. If you find agreement about some aspect of their concern, that is like declaring "no contest" in a court of law—neither guilty nor innocent. Every subject you discuss during this part of the sales process will either lead the buyer closer to a *yes* or distract him farther away from a *yes*. The better move is to remain focused on subjects that will lead the buyer back to another moment of decision.

It's time to put your new knowledge into action. Using the examples above as a guide, write down three concerns you frequently hear from your potential clients. Underneath, write down an aspect of the buyers' concerns that you can agree with, even if you do not agree with their overall concern.

Concern #1:
Agreement:
Concern #2:
Agreement:
Concern #3:
Agreement:

On a more serious note, there is one type of concern on which you should not seek to find agreement. On rare occasions, integrity concerns are spoken of or implied by potential clients. These clients may question your own integrity or the integrity of your company. As a person of integrity, selling for a quality company, you should rarely encounter this type of concern. When you do, remain calm. In a professional manner, refute the potential client immediately. Some things in life are worth standing up for. If a potential client slights your character and you ignore the charge, she may perceive that you are in some measure admitting to her claim. Even if she accuses your company and not you personally, what does it imply about you if you knowingly work for a dishonest company?

An effective way to refute an integrity concern is to use the buyer's own words. Here are some examples:

Buyer: *"Your company makes products that are designed to break down."*

Salesperson: *"My company does not make products that are designed to break down."*

Buyer: *"You are overcharging me."*

Salesperson: *"We are not overcharging you."*

The key to the effectiveness of these statements is *how* you say them. Look the buyer in the eyes. Calmly, yet firmly, refute her charge in her own words. Do not explain anything else, because you cannot explain integrity.

Many potential clients are simply blowing off steam. Most times, when they realize they have questioned your integrity, they back down. They may still have a question about product life or pricing, but now the conversation shifts from integrity to typical sales-related questions. On some occasions, you may actually gain a slight advantage because the potential client, whose words were fueled by emotions that are unrelated to the sale, will feel bad for questioning your integrity.

If the potential client does not back down, the sales appointment is over, anyway. How can you do business with someone who thinks you or your company is dishonest? Find other potential clients who believe in your integrity and that of your company.

189

STEP 4: CONFIRM THAT BUYERS HAVE STATED ALL OF THEIR CONCERNS

Why is it important to confirm that your buyer has asked all his questions and expressed all his concerns?

First, by asking, you remain in control of the conversation. Because making decisions is uncomfortable, many of your buyers will do almost anything to avoid another moment of decision. For example, they will continue to think of more questions that move the conversation farther away from another uncomfortable moment of decision.

Second, you help your buyer organize his thoughts. You just finished your presentation, which was full of new information. Asking the buyer to verbalize the questions he still has helps him organize his thoughts about taking action on your proposal.

Third, identifying all the buyer's questions and concerns at one time helps you avoid a game of question-and-answer ping-pong where the buyer asks questions and you answer them. Average salespeople view the buyer's questions as a sign that they are moving toward the sale—and they may be. However, in the selling game whoever is asking the questions is in control.

Remember: a website can answer questions. You are paid to *persuade* buyers to take immediate action. So gather all the concerns you can before you begin providing answers. "Is this your only concern, or are there other issues we must discuss before you are ready to move forward? And please, be very candid with me."

If you sense that your buyer has other concerns that need to be addressed before he will take immediate action, encourage him to tell you more. "My job is to make sure all your questions are answered. What other concerns might you have?" Patiently continue to ask for his concerns until you sense he has gotten everything out in the open.

What do you do when the buyer still does not say what is stopping him from taking immediate action? Two strategies will encourage the buyer to share the real reason he hesitates to say *yes*. The first strategy is to quickly review the four discovery questions you asked before the presentation.

1. "Earlier, you mentioned there is no one else you need to speak with to make a decision. Is that correct?"
2. "And you mentioned that you have the ability to make a decision today if you desired, correct?"
3. "You also mentioned that the funds to make this purchase are available today. Isn't that right?"
4. "Finally, you mentioned that the quality of this product is an important consideration. For the value I have presented today, is the investment a concern to you?"

Remain relaxed while you review the discovery questions. This isn't an interrogation. You are the buyer's consultant and you are helping him reach an informed decision. Watch carefully as he responds to each question. If he seems uncertain in a particular area, encourage him to talk about it; for example, "It seems like the investment may still be a concern for you."

The second strategy is to move ahead with the fifth and final step in this part of the sales process. If the buyer balks at this next step, it will provide another opportunity to return to this step and discuss other unspoken concerns that keep him from saying *yes*.

STEP 5: CONFIRM THE BUYER'S READINESS TO TAKE ACTION

In the previous step, you confirmed that the buyer has expressed all his questions and concerns. That is a great start, but that alone may not be enough, because you could do a great job responding to his concerns and he still won't say *yes*. Therefore, the final step *before* you begin addressing his concerns is to discover how he will respond *after* you satisfactorily address his concerns.

"If I can adequately address your concern(s)...then would you be ready to move forward with the purchase?"

Word that question whatever way it feels most comfortable for you or as appropriate for your specific industry. Notice that the *if-then* format is a trial close question. You are not asking him to buy. You are asking *if you met the condition* (adequately addressing his concerns), then *would he be ready to take immediate action?* The buyer may hem and haw a bit. That is okay. Take a deep breath, relax, and remain silent until the buyer answers.

What will this question achieve? Before you have spoken the first word in response to his concerns, your buyer has confirmed that after you satisfactorily address his concerns, he will be ready to take action.

Even if he does not agree to take action, your question will move the sale forward, because you will learn more about where he is in the decision-making process. His answer creates an opportunity for you to return to step four and ask, "What other concerns need to be addressed before you are ready to make a purchase?"

Is it possible that the buyer will think of additional concerns after he said he already told you all of them? Yes. Part of the adventure of a sales appointment is that anything can happen. Remain professional and go through the five steps in this chapter again, concluding with this final step: ask your buyer again whether, if you address this new concern, he will be ready to move forward.

It may become apparent that the buyer's challenge is making decisions about *any* matter. Or the buyer may begin to give excuses such as "I want to think about it," or "I don't make quick decisions." In either scenario, you would introduce the ultimate question, which will be discussed in chapter 14.

Now it is time to put your persuasive skills into action by writing down three concerns you hear most frequently and creating your *if-then* trial close questions. The value of writing down these key *if-then* statements and practicing them out loud is that you won't hesitate during this part of the sale. The buyer is filled with hesitation. At this point in the sale, he needs certainty. Your confident delivery of your *if-then* statements will lead him a step closer to the next moment of decision by helping him realize that his concerns are all that is stopping him from saying *yes*. Below are examples:

Concern: "The competition offered a lower price."

If-then: "If I can demonstrate to your satisfaction the value of our services in relation to your investment, then would you be ready to take the next step forward?"

Concern: "I need the products more quickly than you can deliver."

If-then: "If I can show you how we will deliver your products within the time frame you need, then will you be ready to give us a try?"

Multiple concerns: "I'm not sure your products will make much of a difference from our current supplier, and right now we are just too busy to make a switch."

If-then: "If I demonstrated to you that my products will make a significant difference and showed you how quickly you could make the switch, then would you be open to using our line of products?"

Now write three concerns you hear most often, followed by your *if-then* statement:

Concern #1:
If-then:
Concern #2:
If-then:

Concern #3:

If-then:

There is no substitute for practice. You use different parts of your brain for mentally rehearsing and verbally rehearsing the phrases you use during a sales presentation. To become your very best requires both types of practice. Practice with others. If you are alone, make an audio recording with your smartphone and review it.

These five steps meld into one fluid part of the sales process. Use them well, and your buyer will listen attentively to the answers you'll develop in chapter 13.

CHAPTER 12 KEY POINTS

- Keep asking until you discover all the questions and concerns that stop the buyer from saying *yes*.
- Just because the buyer asks questions or raises concerns does not mean you need to respond right away!
- Always listen with the intention of understanding.
- Buyers do not always say what they mean.
- An effective way to refute an integrity concern is to use the buyer's own words.
- Before answering any questions, confirm that the buyer has given you all his concerns.
- Use *if-then* questions to determine how ready your buyer is to buy.

13. Presenting Answers

The Circle of Persuasion

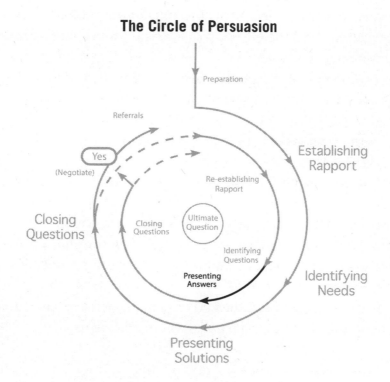

As you journey to the next stop on the inner Circle of Persuasion, consider that presenting answers in response to the questions and concerns of buyers is really a series of short presentations.

These presentations will only take a fraction of the time that your earlier presentation took, but the purpose and methodology is the same. You are providing key information necessary for the buyer to take immediate action and say *yes*. In the outer circle, you gave a full presentation that covered a wide scope of your company's history and credibility as well as your products. Now you are presenting narrow slices of information about your product as defined by the buyer's specific questions or concerns.

The big question at this step in the sales process is: how much information do you give? Give only as much information as the buyer needs to make decisions. Too much information may bring up topics that lead the buyer farther astray rather than closer to making a buying decision.

Unfortunately, many salespeople respond to buyers with the intention of merely answering their questions but gaining no ground toward closing the sale. At this point in the sale, the purpose of the responses is to lead the buyer to another moment of decision. So, after answering, confirm that the response has provided the buyer with the information she needs to make a buying decision.

You may ask, "Did that answer your question? Great. Given that information, does it make more sense now to move ahead with the paperwork?" Or, "Does that additional information make it easier for you to take the next step?"

Trial close questions at the end of your response to the buyer's questions and concerns accomplish three objectives:

1. Trial close questions make sure that you have adequately addressed the buyer's questions and concerns. **Do not assume that your response, which may make perfect sense to you, is a sufficient response to your buyer.** Maybe she didn't hear your words clearly. Maybe she was thinking about something else. Maybe she feels your response didn't address her concern at all.

You won't know if you have accomplished this objective until you confirm the value of your response with her. Because her agreement is a critical factor in proceeding to the next moment of decision, it is worth the time to check.

2. Trial close questions can create a natural transition to the next moment of decision. When the buyer agrees that you have adequately addressed her questions and concerns, she has cleared a path for you to request immediate action—in effect, to ask her to make the buying decision.

3. Trial close questions help you avoid slipping back into wait-and-see selling by keeping you focused on your objective of bringing the buyer back to another moment of decision.

What do you do when the buyer raises multiple questions and concerns? After addressing each question or concern, confirm with the buyer that your response was adequate, but don't tie your response in to the next moment of decision until the last concern has been addressed. The conversation, minus the content of your response, could go something like this:

"You mentioned several important concerns. Let's take them one at a time. In regard to... [give your response]. Does that address your concern in that area? [Yes.] Great, you also had a question about... [give your response]. Did that answer your question? [Yes.]"

On it goes until you address the final concern: "We have addressed all the issues that you mentioned. What other concerns do we need to discuss before moving forward? [None.] Great. Then the next step is..."

Now you can lead them to the next moment of decision, which will be covered in detail in chapter 14.

COMMON SENSE REMINDERS WHEN ADDRESSING CONCERNS AND QUESTIONS

1. Never take the questions and concerns of buyers personally. Many buyers hesitate to make buying decisions. It's not a reflection on your ability to sell. Rather they're probably just not great decision makers. Understanding and working with this knowledge creates the opportunity for you to earn a great income.

2. Never speak poorly about your competition. If the only way you can lift yourself up is to knock someone else down, you're in the wrong business. Demonstrating professionalism will always be more persuasive than speaking down about the competition. If you have a legitimate concern about the safety or financial well-being of potential clients who do business with another company, encourage them to thoroughly check out the other company and just leave it at that.

3. Embrace questions and concerns with appreciation. It is better for buyers to tell you what is stopping them from saying *yes*, even if it is not always pleasant, than for them to remain silent and leave you guessing about how to best persuade them to own your product.

4. Avoid telling buyers they are wrong or that they don't understand.

> **Buyer:** *"I understand this product can run on 110 volts or 220 volts, right?"*
> *Avoid saying, "That is incorrect. It doesn't run on 220 volts."*
> *Instead, say, "The product is designed to run on 110 volts. However we have an adapter available that allows this product to run on 220 volts."*

That example is obvious, right? Unfortunately, there is a more subtle, insidious way to tell buyers they are wrong, which is commonly used by salespeople. It is a word pattern that most frequently occurs in this part of the sales process. You will recognize it the instant you see it: "Yes, but..."

It starts off so nicely. *Yes*... a word of agreement. The very word you wish to hear from your buyer. And then comes trouble with the word *but*. The destructive aspects of this word pattern are found in the word *but*, which negates everything before it.

For example, someone says to you, "Those are great-looking shoes, but they don't match the rest of your outfit." The word *but* negates the compliment about your shoes and says you made the wrong choice in wearing them. Do you like when people tell you that you are wrong? No. Buyers don't like it, either. *Yes, but*... is less abrasive than directly telling someone they are wrong, but the message is the same: "You are wrong."

The *Yes, but*... word pattern is easy to understand in examples when one person says both sides of the sentence. The subtle application to sales occurs when a buyer makes a statement and the salesperson continues the statement with "Yes, but..." The buyer says, "I think it is best to wait until I have enough money to pay cash for your product." The salesperson responds with "Yes, but if you buy it now, you will enjoy the reduction in overhead expenses more quickly." The "but" spoken by the salesperson negates the buyer's statement and indirectly says that wanting to wait until the buyer has enough money to pay cash is... wrong.

Yes, but... builds walls of resentment. Nobody likes to be told, directly or subtly, that they are wrong. Instead, use questions and concerns to build bridges of agreement. When you replace the word *but* with the word *and*, your buyers will respond more favorably. You will still steer the conversation in the opposite direction, in a more pleasing manner, that can take buyers one step closer to the next moment of decision.

5. Avoid telling buyers what you can't do or don't know. Instead, tell them what you *can* do.

> **Buyer:** *"Can you extend the warranty an extra year?"*
> Avoid saying, *"I'm sorry, but we can't extend the warranty."*
> Instead say, *"When you handle your initial order with cash, I can extend your warranty an extra six months."*

6. When you don't know the answer to a question, let the buyer know you will find out and get back to her. Buyers do not expect you to know the answer to every obscure question.

> **Buyer:** *"What if an El Niño storm causes a flood on the second Friday of a thirty-day month?"*
> **Salesperson:** *"That's a really good question that I haven't heard before. Let me check on that and get back to you as quickly as possible."*

7. Never argue with customers or show anger. If the conversation becomes nonproductive, use the ultimate question covered in chapter 14.

Now you have responded to the buyers' questions and concerns. You have re-presented the information they need to make buying decisions. You have taken them back to a moment of decision. What do you do next? You do the same thing you did at the end of your outer circle presentation. You ask them to take action…again.

CHAPTER 13 KEY POINTS

- Your responses to the buyers' questions and concerns are really short presentations.

- Trial close questions make sure that you have adequately addressed the buyer's questions and concerns.
- Never speak poorly about your competition.
- Avoid telling buyers that they are wrong or that they don't understand.
- Don't argue with buyers.

14. The Key Moment of Asking for the Sale

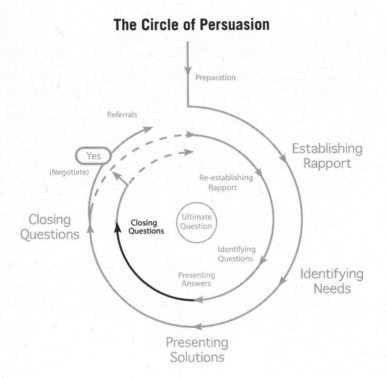

The Circle of Persuasion

Preparation

Referrals

Yes

(Negotiate)

Re-establishing Rapport

Establishing Rapport

Closing Questions

Closing Questions

Ultimate Question

Identifying Questions

Presenting Answers

Identifying Needs

Presenting Solutions

Once again, we are at a point in the sale where the buyer has the information necessary to make an educated decision. At this point, you've identified some needs that weren't addressed during your journey around the outer Circle of Persuasion. You've given acceptable answers to all of the buyer's questions. And, you've covered all the pertinent money issues related to the sale. Now it's time to perform the final and most important step in the inner circle.

Whenever you finish addressing questions and concerns, *always end by asking the buyers to take immediate action*. For most salespeople, that is asking for the sale. For those who are involved in a multistep sale, it is asking the buyer to take the next step.

As covered in chapter 10, you can never assume a buyer will take action. You must always ask—clearly and directly—for the action you want him to take once you have answered all his questions and addressed his concerns. This is where you once again take control of where you are in the sales process.

Directly asking for the sale accomplishes several things:

1. It helps the buyer pinpoint where he is in the decision-making process.

As a sales professional, you know that the buyer now has all the information he needs in order to make informed buying decisions. But do not make the assumption that your buyer knows this. You must actively help the buyer realize that he is now at another moment of decision. Remember the three basic selling activities: *making statements*, *asking questions*, *and remaining silent*. Asking a closing question and then remaining silent will very clearly signal to the buyer that he has arrived at another moment of decision.

2. It helps you remain in control of the conversation.

Making money decisions can often make buyers uncomfortable. Their natural inclination may be to avoid decisions that involve them parting with their money or committing their time to something. Because of this, if you do not remain in control of the conversation and keep them focused on this next step in the sales process, buyers may stall and ask more questions or change the subject to avoid the moment of decision.

You are in charge here. Like a medical doctor working with a patient, you decide the course of treatment. Based on the patient's symptoms, you prescribe the appropriate medicine. During a sales appointment, part of the prescription process is helping the buyer to understand that your product or service will relieve his symptoms. Your closing questions tell him when he has arrived at the next moment of decision—to accept your diagnosis and prescribed treatment. Your silence gives him time to make that decision.

When asking the buyer to take action, use words that create mental pictures of what you want him to do, not pictures of what you do not want him to do. Whatever you say, the buyer must mentally process it, however briefly, to make sense of your words. As such, make sure all of your closing questions are filled with positive word pictures of the buyer taking ownership, such as:

move forward	*buying decision*
take the next step	*purchase*
participation	*satisfied*
immediate action	*with your approval*
as my client…	*schedule training*
your warranty includes…	*schedule delivery*

As you practice writing out the last few sentences of your closing call to action, take this list of words and phrases and actively incorporate them into your sales vocabulary.

Many salespeople themselves become uncomfortable during these key moments of decision, because they feel like they're applying pressure or being pushy. In short, they'd rather squirm themselves than watch a buyer squirm over making a decision.

But you have to overcome this hesitancy, because that is exactly what must happen. You are paid to bring the buyer to moments of decision. Some buyers make decisions quickly and calmly. Other buyers wrestle with the process as described above. But both types of buyers need the benefits of your products and services.

Regardless of how they handle making buying decisions, it remains your responsibility as a sales professional to guide buyers through the process. The more difficult that decision-making process is for them, the greater the service you provide to them as a sales professional. You are helping them to find sound solutions to the challenges they are having. You are helping them rationalize owning the benefits of your product or service.

So during those moments when the emotions of decision making are heightened, take in an easy breath, maintain a pleasant expression, and remain quiet. Let the silence do its work.

Once the decision is made, these very same buyers will love you for helping them through the decision-making process. As a person of integrity selling for a company that offers valuable products and services, you will become one of their trusted business advisors in your area of expertise. The tougher the buyers are to close, the more loyal they will become once you do a good job of serving their needs. Keep that in mind when you're remaining quiet and allowing the buyer to make his decision.

Do you see how the process you follow in the inner circle is more enjoyable and profitable than making a presentation, answering a barrage of questions, and then waiting to see what the buyer does next? This is why top-performing salespeople find sales interesting, fun, and profitable. They take the necessary actions throughout the sales process to increase the probability of a *yes* response from their buyers.

IF THEY NEED A LITTLE MORE ENCOURAGEMENT

What do you do when you have addressed all the questions and concerns, asked the buyer to make a decision, and remained silent... but your buyer still won't take immediate action? The buyer doesn't ask you to leave, yet she doesn't authorize your written sales agreement. What's next?

The Circle of Persuasion

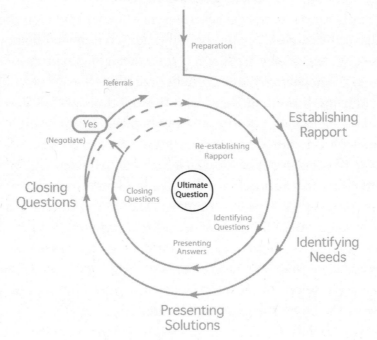

When you believe you have given the buyers all the information they need to make informed decisions and there is nothing more to be discussed, it is time to ask the ultimate question. The ultimate question will put a stop to going round in circles with people you know would benefit from your product but who just won't make a commitment.

What is the ultimate question you can ask your buyer to take her from no action to immediate action? It would be something along the lines of this: "What needs to happen for you to take the next step today?" Or, "What else can I do today to help you start enjoying the benefits of this widget that you seem to like so much?" Use your own words, but be prepared to ask. Otherwise, you and the buyer could end up rehashing the same topics until cobwebs take over.

Now, the most important word in the ultimate question is *today*. What needs to happen *today* for the buyer to say *yes*? Not next week. Not when they are feeling more comfortable about making a buying decision. *Today*, what would need to happen for the buyer to make a buying decision?

As with any other closing question, remain silent after you ask. The first person who talks owns the product. If it's you, the product will likely stay in your hands or in your company's warehouse. But when the buyer speaks first, she is either going to own it herself or give you a reason why she's not ready. Either way, you're still in the game.

The ultimate question is an open-ended question that requires the buyer to use her imagination to identify a solution that allows her to say *yes*. Often, you will be pleasantly surprised by the answers your buyer comes up with.

"I could use the company credit card."

"If I can reach the owner by phone, she may give approval."

"I will put half down today if I can pay the balance in thirty days."

"Perhaps the purchasing manager can authorize this."

"If you invoice us in January, we could put this in next year's budget."

If the buyer does not agree with the solution you have presented, or raises another concern, restate the ultimate question.

You wouldn't be quite this blunt, but the point of your ultimate question is this: "You like these features and you want these benefits. What is the reason you are not taking action now?" Craft your ultimate question carefully using your own words, but do prepare to use it.

Using a baseball analogy, this final question is a free swing of the bat. You have devoted your time and energy to meeting with the buyer. You have asked every question and delivered every statement needed for the buyer to make an educated decision. Now you are using an open-ended question to give your buyer one last chance to brainstorm how she might make the purchase today. Put the same effort into creating your ultimate question as you did in preparing the rest of your presentation, and you'll get more *yes*es.

At the very least, the ultimate question will open up the door to a possible negotiation situation with your buyer. That sometimes does occur. She may answer with what-if types of questions such as:

- "What if I were to order three widgets instead of two? Would you be able to come down on your unit price?"
- "What if we needed to spread the investment out over a longer time period?"

When buyers respond with anything other than "I can't really think of any way we could do this," rest assured the sales process has not ended. It has just taken a detour into negotiation, which will be covered in the next two chapters.

WHEN NO TRULY MEANS NO

How do you conclude your sales appointment when all avenues have been exhausted and the buyer still has not made a commitment to go ahead? Before you leave a nonsale situation, be sure to do the following:

a) Concisely state:

- the customer's wishes / issues,
- your company's solution,
- the reason the buyer has said she is not taking action, and
- the consequences of not taking action.

b) Ask the ultimate question one last time.

Your goal here is to know more ways of asking for the sale than the buyer knows how to say *no*. "What can we do to get you started with our solution today?" Every once in a while, the buyer will realize the selling game has come to an end, and she will start having second thoughts about losing out on the solution you presented. In some cases, asking one more time is just enough to get her off the fence.

c) Assure your buyer you are always there to help, even if it's not today.

You have journeyed all this way with your buyer. During the sales appointment, you learned more about her than most of her other vendors have. Do not burn the bridges that you have built. Assure your buyer of your role as a consultant for that day in the future when she *is* ready to find a solution for her challenges.

d) Know in your heart that you have done your best.

Any time you have followed all the steps in the Circle of Persuasion, you should feel *great* about the professional way you worked with the buyer. If a buying decision cannot or will not be made that day, schedule a follow-up contact. If your buyer won't agree to meeting again, ask for permission to make a follow-up call. Even if her response is vague, now is the best time to set her expectations for your follow-up contacts. Keep the door open. You never know when she will change her mind or have her circumstances change in the future. In the meantime, spend your time with buyers who are ready to buy now.

Be confident in every sales scenario:

- When buyers have questions, educate them with product knowledge.
- When buyers misunderstand, discover the source of the misunderstanding and clarify the information.
- When buyers are upset, politely seek to understand why.
- If buyers question the integrity of your company, calmly refute them using the same words they use.
- When buyers hesitate, make it easy to take the next step.
- When buyers procrastinate, explain the disadvantages of waiting.
- When you are not sure of an answer, set a time to reconnect with the best solution.

Because you are a student of persuasion, you enjoy the confidence of knowing you will soon close another sale. A nonsale is not the end of the road for you. In fact, you have probably learned some valuable lessons from it that you can carry forward in your career.

In the selling scenarios below, you will find examples of using the four steps of the inner Circle of Persuasion.

Scenario 1: Business Sales Appointment

Kate finishes her presentation and asks Mr. Stevens to take action. After a moment of thought, he says, "We're in the middle of our busy season right now. I'm not sure it is a good time to switch. I'm not getting reliable service now, but for the price it's been getting us by."

Kate waits to make sure he has finished verbalizing his concerns. "I am glad that you raised those two important considerations. To make sure we are on the same page," she replies, using words that matched his feeling words, "you are concerned about upgrading your widgets in the middle of your busy season?"

"Yes. One of the teams is tied up in a long-term project for the next several months. The other team is traveling on short notice to service one of our clients' unexpected needs."

Then Kate rewords Mr. Stevens's indirect concern about price and getting by on his current equipment. "And you have a question about the difference in value between the services of Widget Corp and your current provider?"

"I wouldn't put it that way," Mr. Stevens says with a grin. He wants to lighten the conversation as they continue moving away from the moment of decision.

She smiles at his humor and continues. "Dean, I'll address these two questions in a second. Is there anything else that we need to discuss before you are ready to upgrade your widgets?"

"No, not really."

Kate isn't excited to hear the "not really," but with two of Mr. Stevens's concerns in play, she decides to continue. "We certainly agree that it is important to make decisions that support your current busy season. And we both agree that funding is an important consideration when making an investment in your company. So if I can address these two concerns in a satisfactory manner, then you would be okay with moving forward today on upgrading your unreliable widgets?"

"That's a big if," he says jokingly about the challenging nature of his concerns.

"I understand. And if I can, then you are ready to move forward, right?"

Mr. Stevens shrugs. "Sure."

"That's great." Kate picks up her tablet and moves to the page in her electronic presentation that shows the capabilities of Widget Corp's online training program and twenty-four-hour support line. "Given that your traveling teams can access our online support from anywhere in the world via the Internet, does that alleviate your concerns about your teams quickly getting up to speed on the new widgets during the busy season?"

Mr. Stevens considers her words. "My boys are pretty independent when it comes to figuring out the challenges on a job. So if they have access to the information, they could quickly make the changes."

"Would you agree that Widget Corp can quickly deliver that support to your teams when needed?"

"Sure."

His nonchalant agreement convinces Kate that Mr. Stevens is on board in this area. "Now for the elephant in the room," Kate begins. Mr. Stevens laughs, as she intended. "After what we discussed during the presentation about the quality of products and services offered by Widget Corp, do you really believe that the local independent companies give the same level of service?"

"Well, I like the Widget Corp name, but really…" Wanting to be polite, Mr. Stevens fudges on his answer.

She asked the question to introduce doubt, not to elicit a particular response. She could explain many features that provide value, but first she wants to give Mr. Stevens some additional motivation for choosing a value-based company over a price-based company. "We provide value in many ways that our lower-cost competitors do not. Do you keep a copy of your widget agreement here in your office?"

"Yes," he answers warily.

"Would you please take a moment to look at it?" She quickly adds, "I don't need to see it. I am familiar with ABC Widgets' agreement."

Indeed she is. As Mr. Stevens asks his assistant to bring in a copy of his current agreement, she remembers the hours of time she spent reviewing all of her competitors' written agreements. She learned all the small-print details where the price-based companies cut corners. In fact, in the file box in her car, she has a copy of an ABC Widgets' agreement.

When his assistant brings in a copy of the agreement, Kate continues. "Look on page two. Should be the third or fourth paragraph down. You will see the section on insurance. You may be interested in reading what it says."

Thirty seconds of silence are broken by Mr. Stevens's voice. "What?! I'm not naming them additional insured. And I'm certainly not going to hold them harmless regardless of their actions. What kind of company expects you to hold them harmless even if they caused the problem? Why did we agree—" He flips to the date on the final page. His voice

213

returns to normal volume. "Oh, I remember. We were in danger of losing a huge account in Canada. I was out of the country when our agreement expired. I told my office manager to handle it. I guess I didn't carefully read the agreement when I returned. Hmm." He sets the agreement down. "Well, that's good to know. There's no clause like this in your contract, right?"

Kate looks directly into his eyes. "We believe that if we create a situation, then we should be responsible. If you create a situation, then you should be responsible."

Mr. Stevens nods. "I believe that, too."

Kate believes she scored big points on that. Mr. Stevens understands the insurance liability, and she thinks it is time for the second close. "So you now have additional information that addresses your two concerns. Does that make it easier for you to move forward today?"

"Yes, it does."

"Great," Kate says with a smile. "Let's get started with the paperwork."

Mr. Stevens furrows his brow and stares at the ceiling. "If I buy more than one widget, what type of discount would I get?"

His negotiation request is not the response Kate desires, but she welcomes it as being one step closer to getting a *yes* . . .

Scenario 2: Residential Sales Appointment

Bob is using the paperwork close to move Pat and Gary to a moment of decision. Gary hesitates, and then Pat raises the question, "I'm not very good at learning about these sorts of things. What if something happens to Gary?"

The moment of decision ends, and Bob shifts to the first step in the inner circle without missing a beat. "I'm so glad you brought that up. I meant to cover that in greater detail during my presentation."

Pat feels sheepish for admitting her limited knowledge about widgets, but she visibly relaxes when Bob affirms her concern as an important question.

He continues by restating her question to make sure he understands what she is asking. "You are asking what you would do to benefit from your widget if something happened to Gary?"

"Yes," Pat replies.

"Now before I get to that, what other concerns or questions do we need to discuss before you are ready to take the next step in getting your widget?"

Pat does not seem to have any further questions. Bob looks at Gary and waits. Gary shifts in his chair. "I'm not sure this is a good time."

To confirm that he understands, Bob restates Gary's statement. "You are not sure if it is better to act now or later?"

"I guess."

"Timing is an important consideration. Let's discuss that. What other questions or concerns do we need to discuss before you are ready to move forward?"

Pat and Gary shrug.

"Okay," Bob continues. "So if I satisfactorily address Pat's question about knowing how to use the widget and Gary's question about the best time to take action, you would both be ready to move forward today?"

"Probably," Pat says quietly. Gary remains silent.

Bob can easily see Gary's nonverbal hesitation. He asks again for Gary's agreement. "Gary?"

"I don't know...," Gary says quietly, still shaking his head. "I like your product, don't get me wrong. It's just that..."

"What is it, honey?" Pat asks.

"Well, it's Diane's trip this summer. And my busy season doesn't begin until March, at the earliest."

"Our daughter is going to Europe this summer for a study program with the university," Pat explains. "They want the full payment by the end of this month."

"Spending time in Europe sounds exciting," Bob says, using another hearing word.

"So is the price tag," replies Gary. "Sixty-six hundred plus airfare. Both need to be paid this month."

"I'm glad you explained that." Bob really is glad that he finally learned the source of Gary's hesitation. "So with payment on Diane's trip due this month, you are concerned about cash flow?"

Gary nods.

"Well, I certainly agree on the wisdom of planning your cash flow. Is this your only concern, or are there other issues we must discuss before you are ready to move forward?"

Gary looks at Pat and says, "I think that's it. It makes sense for us to be careful during our slow season."

"Great. So if I can adequately address your concern about cash flow during your slow season, then would you be ready to move forward this evening?"

Gary nods, but Bob interprets his nonverbal communication as noncommittal. Unsatisfied, Bob presses for a verbal response. If Gary does not agree that this is the only concern preventing him from taking immediate action, then responding to his concern will not lead to the next closing moment. Bob smiles. He is about to cash in the rapport capital he has built so far during the sales appointment. "Gary," he begins in an understanding voice, "are there other concerns that we need to discuss besides cash flow?"

"No," Gary says, this time more definitively.

"I realize cash flow is an important concern to you both," Bob says, including Pat at the end of his statement to take some of the spotlight off Gary, "so if I can adequately address your concerns about cash flow, would you be ready to move forward today?"

Bob maintains his pleasant expression and continues to match Gary's posture. The anxiety of decision-making is in the air, and it is evident on Gary's face. Once again, Pat looks at Gary.

"Yes," Gary says tersely.

Enthusiasm creeps into Bob's voice as he says, "I have some solutions you may find quite attractive." He picks up the Residential Widgets brochure from the kitchen table, once again fully exposing the written agreement. Bob opens the brochure to the page that shows Residential Widgets' support line center, where their trained staff walks customers through each step of using a widget. Gary switches his cell phone to speakerphone mode and calls the support line center. A woman's friendly voice answers and Gary introduces Pat. The call line specialist gives a brief sixty-second overview of how the support line center helps customers quickly get up to speed on using a widget. Gary ends the call, and Pat's beaming smile shows her response. "That was great. Thank you," she says with enthusiasm.

Satisfied that Pat's concern has been addressed, Bob

turns to Gary. Over the next few minutes, he explains in detail the Residential Widgets' financing program. When Gary demurs at the idea of going into debt, Bob mentions the option of paying one-third down now, one-third when the widget arrives in March, and the balance thirty days after that. Gary seems receptive to that option, and Bob decides it is time to close again. "Does that option address your concerns about cash flow between now and your busy season?"

"That does make it easier," Gary says, casting a glance at Pat.

"So what we are talking about is one-third as an initial investment," Bob summarizes as he picks up the written agreement. He turns to the final page and begins writing in a blank box in the "Conditions" section. "One-third down. Another third when you receive your widget. The final third thirty days after that."

Out of the corner of his eye, Bob can see Gary and Pat silently communicating with each other. He continues looking at the written agreement for a few seconds to give them extra time. When he looks up, he begins the final part of his close. "So if that makes sense to you, let's put the rest of the information down on the paperwork."

Several moments of silence pass. Bob is relaxed and has no intention of speaking until one of them replies. Pat begins to fidget, but Gary remains still as he looks at the dates on the agreement for each one-third amount. Finally he shakes his head. "The payments are too close together. Can we have sixty days between payments instead of thirty days?"

Inwardly, Bob smiles as Gary's negotiation request moves them nearer to the next moment of decision...

CHAPTER 14 KEY POINTS

- You must always ask—clearly and directly—for the action you want the buyer to take.
- When asking the buyer to take action, use words that create positive mental images of what you want him to do.
- It's always critically important to ask the ultimate question before giving up on the sale.
- Ultimate questions open up the door to potential negotiations.
- If a buying decision cannot or will not be made, schedule your follow-up contact.

15. Preparing for Negotiation Requests

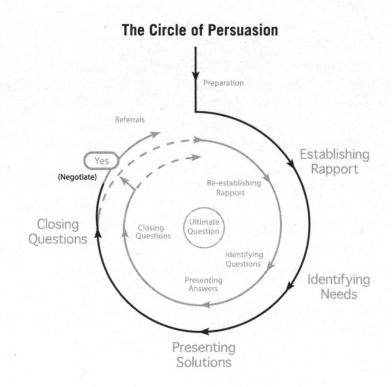

The Circle of Persuasion

Preparation

Referrals

Yes

(Negotiate)

Re-establishing
Rapport

Establishing
Rapport

Closing
Questions

Closing
Questions

Ultimate
Question

Identifying
Questions

Identifying
Needs

Presenting
Answers

Presenting
Solutions

Negotiation is an important yet frequently neglected part of selling. As a result, salespeople sometimes become involved in negotiations with their buyers but don't even realize what's happened. Buyers make negotiation requests, and salespeople—still in the mind-set of responding to concerns—mistake the negotiation requests for more concerns to address.

While the two often sound similar, there is a profound distinction.

When buyers raise *objections* or *concerns*, they indicate that they will not do business with you until the concerns have been adequately addressed. **When buyers present *negotiation requests*, they indicate that they want to do business with you…but with different terms.**

Most often, their requests concern the financial investments, value, or time constraints, such as:

- They want to pay less for your product or service.
- They want to receive more value for your stated price.
- They want a time consideration: overnight delivery, work completed by a certain date, work done during certain hours, or to make the payments over time.

Negotiation requests can come at any time during a sales appointment. Often they come when you least expect them. You're talking about one subject, and suddenly the buyer will make a negotiation request about a completely different subject.

Buyer: *"Can you include that demo model for free?"*
Salesperson: *"You mean the $2,500 demo model I am showing you right now?"*
Buyer: *"Yep. It's used, right?"*

Seriously…buyers will ask:

"Can I get an extra month's online support included for free?"
"Can you extend the warranty an extra year as part of a package?"
"Can I pay half down now and the balance upon delivery?"

Those are examples that assume the unmentioned first part of their sentence, which is "If I buy from you..." Notice how those three examples alter your perception when restated with the *unmentioned* assumption.

"If I buy this from you, can I get an extra month's online support included for free?"

"If I purchase this product from you, can you extend the warranty an extra year as part of a package?"

"If I am able to come up with the money to buy this from you, can I pay half down now and the balance upon delivery?"

Keep the phrase *If I purchase* in the forefront of your mind during your sales presentations. If it fits well on the front of a question your buyer asks, she's asking you to negotiate.

Now compare those negotiation requests to these *concerns*:

"This costs too much."

"I have to think about it."

"We're happy with our current suppliers."

These concerns indicate that the buyer *has not* found agreement with you on the investment, the need to take immediate action, or the value of your product. That is significantly different from when the buyer asks you about terms of sale.

So the first step in a negotiation is recognizing when your buyer has initiated one.

A negotiation request is a closing question *from your buyer*! Sometimes the buyer's negotiation request comes in the form of a direct close:

"Will you include an extra widget in the deal?"

"Will you lower your price by 10 percent?"

Sometimes the buyer's negotiation request comes in the form of a trial close:

"If I were to buy today, would you include a widget in the sale?"
"If I were to buy several units, would you lower your price by 10 percent?"

As stated above, buyers often omit the opening phrase *If I were to buy.* You must listen carefully to catch their subtle signals. Your buyer is attempting to close you! Yes, you have to find agreement on the pesky terms of the sale, but isn't that a more enjoyable, profitable task than trying to warm up a frowning buyer who objects that your product costs too much? Some salespeople resent negotiation requests, especially when those requests come right at the end of the sales appointment. They especially resent negotiation requests when buyers are responsive and it looks like they are about to close the sale. Then comes the request for more:

"Can I get a 10 percent quantity discount?"
"Can you include an extra widget?"
"Can you deliver by seven in the morning?"

Never fear! Negotiation requests are actually great buying signs! They mean your buyer is considering the possibility of owning and she is trying to work out the details in a manner that makes sense to her or makes her feel more comfortable. You have successfully taken your buyer off the fence of indecision. You still have to do some work to close the sale, but the odds have significantly shifted in your favor.

FOUR STEPS OF PREPARATION

Preparing for a negotiation means preparing for the possibility that during any sales appointment, the buyer may ask you to alter the terms of sale. You don't know which terms of sale they will ask you to modify or when they will make their negotiation requests. However, by determining your parameters in the four areas discussed below, you will be fully prepared.

This chapter and the next are not meant to be an exhaustive look at negotiation strategies that detail complex negotiations most salespeople never encounter. Instead, they are designed to explain the foundational elements involved in every sales negotiation.

Know your starting point

The first step in preparing for a negotiation is to determine your starting point. What is the best investment and what is the best package of features that you will present to the buyer to start a negotiation? If your pricing is set by your company, that simplifies things. But if you have any flexibility in determining the investment for your products, then you can choose what type of profit margin and features to include.

Factors for choosing your starting point in a negotiation include:

a) How much profit does your company need in order to remain a sustainable business?

Most companies have minimum profit requirements as well as sales revenue requirements. If you lower the amount enough and add enough extra features, you can sell pretty much anything. It's sad but true that some salespeople can make sales only by giving too much away. However, they may kill the goose that gives them the golden eggs of income.

If you frequently lower your prices below the amount needed by your company to make enough profit to remain sustainable, your sales revenues will eventually be viewed as a liability, and you may find yourself making a career adjustment. It's wiser and healthier for your bank account to improve your selling skills instead.

b) How much do you personally need to sell in order to qualify for your quotas and bonuses?

You want to create a win-win for your clients and your company, but you also have the responsibility to make enough income to take care of yourself and your loved ones. Remain aware of how close you are to meeting your quotas and qualifying for bonuses. Sometimes a few more orders can lead to a lot more income, and your improved negotiating skills can make that happen.

c) As best you can, determine if your buyer is a negotiator.

Some buyers feel it's their obligation to negotiate in order to feel good about any purchase. The first time you do business with a buyer, this may be a challenge to determine. For example, you work your numbers for price concessions and extra value. You enthusiastically go to the buyer and exclaim, "Look at how low I got this for you!"

The buyer says, *"So that's your best price?"*

You gasp. *"No, you don't understand. I saved us both time and worked this down to my very best price already. This is 10 percent less than I've received permission to sell this product ever before!"*

The buyer says, *"That's great. Can you give me 5 percent more off if I pay cash?"*

You take in a deep breath. *"This is my very best price. I did the negotiating in advance for you and got an amount that you could never get by going to my company directly or through the company reps. This is an awesome investment."*

The buyer nods. *"Call me when you can go lower. In the meantime, I'll keep looking..."*

That scenario needs to happen only once before you learn that some buyers will take immediate action *only* after they have bargained with you. Bargaining is just part of the buying process for them.

As a result, never start with your lowest amount. However, be sure to start with a fair investment, because buyers have a way of knowing when you've suggested a starting amount that is unrealistic. Give buyers a good starting amount, but leave yourself room to negotiate.

Negotiating can rub some salespeople the wrong way. They don't like to waste time in a negotiation when they can simply give their best numbers up front and save everyone's time. If you experience similar feelings, you have two choices:

1. Recognize and accept the starting point of your buyer. Some buyers want to negotiate, and that is part of their buying process. By participating in their buying process, you are helping to serve your buyer's needs.
2. Do not negotiate. Draw a line in the sand at the start and say, "This is my best price. If you want it, that's the amount and terms of sale." That's also a form of negotiation...but okay, you're basically saying to the buyer that the buying process she needs to feel good about doesn't matter to you. In this sale, you would rather have your way and not negotiate (as the buyer defines negotiation) than do business with her.

Know your ending point

How much are you willing to concede in price and value in order to close the sale? Knowing your absolute limits provides you with a surprising amount of peace of mind. If you know how far you can bend, you won't fear bending too far. You avoid the anxiety of closing a sale you are later ashamed of, or of hearing your boss reprimand you for losing the company money. And you can use that knowledge to let your buyer know that at a certain point your hands are tied. You can still be the friendly expert advisor and let "upper management" be viewed as setting very strong pricing guidelines.

It is generally better to err on the side of a higher amount. Remember our discussion in chapter 9 about how to sell value rather than price? Why become entangled in an unprofitable sale that could cause days or weeks of challenges, when you can go out and find another buyer who appreciates and is willing to pay for the value offered by your products?

Make sure there is enough money involved in each transaction. You may be pleasantly surprised to watch how tracking clear objectives draws you toward the achievement of those objectives. Buyers often give you what you ask for.

- If you expect 50 percent down on a large project that costs several hundred thousand dollars, buyers will often give you that.
- If you expect a buyer to take immediate action, he will often make a decision during the sales appointment.

Know what's negotiable

Many salespeople don't negotiate with their buyers, because they do not realize how many negotiable points they have at their command. If your company sets the terms for pricing or offers a limited choice in style, size, or color, it could be easy to assume you and your buyers have few options for negotiating. The fact is that most salespeople *do* have areas in which they can negotiate.

Now is a great time to make a list of what is truly negotiable in your sale. Let's start with the easy items:

- If you sell a product, what are the models, sizes, colors, and other features that are available?
  - Which of those items are requested most by your clients?
  - Which items are the most difficult for your company to produce, either because of the effort needed to produce it or the scarcity of materials to make it?
- If you sell a service, what are the various levels of service you offer?

Next, list your investment options:

- Do you have sales events with lower investments or end-of-the-month specials?
- Do you match competitor pricing?
- Are you or your manager authorized to adjust the amounts charged?
- Can buyers get a discount if they pay cash?
- If buyers purchase with an in-house credit program or a credit card, does that affect price? How does the delivery of your product affect the monies involved?
- Is there a scheduled price increase coming soon?
- Is your pricing directly affected if buyers:
  - request rush orders or delayed orders?
  - purchase multiple items?
  - purchase today rather than next week?
  - put down a deposit and your company holds the order for an amount of time?
  - purchase using an installment plan?

You definitely want to be familiar with every option available from your company.

Other areas where buyers tend to negotiate may include warranty or customer service options:

- Can you adjust the length of the warranty the buyer receives?
- Can you adjust the length of customer support access?
- Are there levels of customer service you can offer in person, over the phone, or online?

Preparation will prevent you from becoming lost in a negotiation with not knowing what action to take next. When a buyer makes a negotiation request and does not agree to your response, you want to have other options to offer. The more options you have, the easier it is to find agreement on a win-win opportunity.

Here's a sample list of negotiable points in a sale:

- guarantee delivery by requested date when they decide today
- scheduling completion of work before the buyer's busy season when he makes a larger initial investment
- extended warranty when the buyer chooses the deluxe model
- higher level of customer support when the buyer purchases multiple items
- free shipping when the buyer purchases today
- lock in delivery date when the buyer invests today
- give a discount when the buyer purchases before the end of the month
- avoid an upcoming fee increase when the buyer approves an agreement and gives an initial investment today
- 10 percent less when the buyer pays 100 percent today
- guarantee availability of your most popular model when the buyer owns today
- free upgrade when the buyer authorizes the paperwork today
- an extra month when the buyer invests in a one-year service agreement

Now it is your turn: what is your written list of negotiable points?

It is advantageous to make a long list, because you never know when one of those points will come in handy. The great news is that from your long list of negotiation points, you will discover that two or three items are the most important to your company and to you.

For example, if you sell a large-ticket item that most buyers own after making several monthly investments, then a concession most advantageous to your company may be asking for a larger initial investment. By increasing the initial amount you receive from buyers, you will reduce your company's receivables. The value of that liquidity to your company may be worth granting the negotiation requests from your buyers. Realizing this, asking for a larger initial amount could be your response to many negotiation requests from your buyers.

Below are three situations where you could use the same negotiation point of a greater initial investment to move the buyer closer to the next moment of decision:

Buyer: *"Can you complete the work by June 1, when our busy season begins?"*

Salesperson: *"To do that, we would have to bring in a team from out of town. My managers would be more willing to cover that extra expense if you* increase your initial investment *to 75 percent."*

Buyer: *"Can you include the deluxe materials in your work instead of the standard materials?"*

Salesperson: *"Because that would involve direct out-of-pocket expenses from our suppliers, it would* require 100 percent down from you.*"*

Buyer: *"Your competitor is charging 15 percent less for the same work. What can you do on price?"*

Salesperson: *"If you are able to* put down 75 percent *on the order, that will give my manager some wiggle room to get closer to the competitor's number."*

The circumstances were different in each sales scenario, yet the same negotiation point was useful in reaching a win-win agreement.

Another example of a frequently used point of negotiation that is useful in multiple selling scenarios is asking the buyer to take immediate action. Below are two selling scenarios in which the same negotiation point of taking immediate action can be used to reach a win-win agreement.

Buyer: *"Can I have an extra year of extended warranty?"*
Salesperson: *"If you are ready to* move forward today, *I will see if my manager would approve that."*

Buyer: *"Can you deliver the product on New Year's Day?"*
Salesperson: *"That will require special arrangements, but if you* authorize the agreement today, *I will have time to get the approvals needed for your request."*

So make a long list of negotiation points, because you never know when a specific negotiation point from your list may be the perfect solution to close a sale. And from that list, be on the lookout for two or three negotiation points that you may use most frequently to close a sale.

Know when to walk away

At some point, it makes sense to walk away from a negotiation. You've reached your bottom line and explored all the options. The buyer just won't budge.

From the company's perspective, there is an opportunity cost to consider. Many companies have only so much capacity at a given moment, in either manufacturing, access to goods, or the ability to provide services. To tie up those precious resources to fulfill a sale with thin margins may cost the company the profits of another opportunity that may come along in the near future.

And from a personal perspective, you also need to decide when to walk away from a sale that does not make sense. As your confidence in your sales abilities and knowledge about your company grow, you will become more aware and more discerning about the types of sales you accept. Maybe you are at a point in your sales career or on an economic cycle where you need every sale you can get. Necessity-driven, break-even sales will not lead you to a profitable sales career. Even worse, they may present temptations to bend your selling ethics.

When you become clear about what types of sales situations make sense for your company or yourself, your buyers will respond to your certainty. When buyers ask if you can lower your price 10 percent and you respond both verbally and nonverbally with an absolute *NO*, they will sense there is no budging on this point.

Another factor to consider about walking away from a negotiation is whether you have to deal with a difficult buyer after the sale. If a sale is extremely profitable, then take the money and take your lumps. But if the sale is a break-even situation, consider whether you want to spend the next days, weeks, or months of your life working with an unpleasant client. The most demanding people—those who haggle you down to the last penny—are usually the least appreciative clients. Hopefully, these types of buyers are the minority in your sales career, but consider this: bullies respect pushback. They don't like it, but they respect it. The more a buyer tries to bully you into granting negotiation requests, the more you need to stand your ground. So be prepared and enjoy the confidence of firmly communicating your boundaries.

THE KEY ADVANTAGES OF PREPARATION

1. Preparation keeps you from promising more than you can deliver. During a fast-paced sales appointment, you can be so focused on closing the sale that you give away more value than makes sense or is necessary. If you had more clearly defined your boundaries in advance, you might have responded differently to the buyer's negotiation requests.

2. Preparation gives you a chance to work with what is really important to the buyer. This allows you the chance to consider several ways to meet the needs of your buyer in ways that are advantageous to you and your company.

3. Preparing for a negotiation frees you to listen more closely to what your buyer is really saying, because you aren't making calculations about what you can or can't negotiate. Missed clues equal missed sales. When you are preoccupied, it is hard to notice the small clues that the buyer gives.

Many salespeople, because of lack of preparation, are wait-and-see negotiators. When a buyer makes a negotiation request, a wait-and-see negotiator rushes to the bottom-line investment, then waits and sees what questions or negotiation requests the buyer will present next. Wait-and-see negotiators are *reactive* instead of *proactive*. But they are *great* to buy from. Just ask and you will receive!

Buyer: *"Can you give me a better price?"*
Wait-and-see salesperson: *"Sure. Does 5 percent less sound better to you?"*
Buyer: *"Yep. How about free shipping?"*

Wait-and-see salesperson: *"I can take care of that."*

Buyer: *"Fantastic. Can you extend the warranty for another year?"*

Wait-and-see salesperson: *"Uh, I'm only allowed to give an extra six-month warranty."*

Buyer: *"I'll take that. Can I put down half now and the rest later?"*

Wait-and-see salesperson: (shrugs) *"Okay."*

Buyer: *"What is your very lowest price…?"*

That's a great sales scenario when you are buying. That's not so great when you are selling. So when you prepare for a negotiation, even for just a few minutes before the sales appointment begins, several good results will occur:

1. You will recognize the negotiation requests of your buyer more quickly.
2. You will better understand the context of the negotiation requests.
3. You will be ready to ask for a concession in return.
4. You will have more confidence to ask for what you want and draw the line when you've conceded all you can give.

The better your buyers are at negotiating, the more they will respect your confidence as a negotiator. Preparation is the path that will lead you to becoming a confident negotiator.

CHAPTER 15 KEY POINTS

- Negotiation requests mean buyers want to do business with you, but under different terms.
- Preparing for a negotiation gives you confidence and wins the respect of your buyers.

- Preparing a written list of negotiation points in advance frees your attention to notice important clues from buyers that will help you close the sale.
- You may use two or three negotiation points from your written list most often.
- Never start a negotiation by offering your lowest possible price.
- Knowing your ending point and when to walk away allows you to set boundaries with confidence.

16. How to Negotiate with Buyers

Now the fun *really* begins. Your buyer presented a negotiation request and the odds have now shifted in your favor. How did that happen? Your buyer has jumped off the fence of indecision and is now actively "trying on" the idea of purchasing your product—with different buying terms, of course. So all of your selling skills must be ready to be used to find agreement with the buyer. Remember, the advantage is yours because you are more prepared for this negotiation than your buyer is.

THE #1 MISTAKE IN NEGOTIATING

What would you guess is the most frequent mistake salespeople make during a negotiation? It's dropping the price too quickly. Salespeople frequently make this mistake because they think, *The reason the buyer hasn't bought yet is that the price is too high. If I lower the price, then she will buy.*

The easiest path of action is always to lower the amount. Lowering the amount may close a few sales, but it may not lead to the best opportunity for your company, nor will it consequently create the most wins for your sales career. Be careful about developing this habit. In the long term it will have a negative effect on your career and income.

How do you avoid the most frequent mistake in negotiating?

The same way you avoid the most frequent mistake in addressing concerns. You treat a negotiation request like a game of chess. Your initial reaction just after the buyer first makes a negotiation request will determine the success of your later actions.

Let's go through the negotiation process step-by-step.

a) Remain relaxed

You are just on the verge of a sale. You made the presentation and asked the buyer to take action. The buyer raised some concerns, but they are the good kind of concerns that are riddled with buying signals. You feel certain you are about to close the sale, and then the buyer says:

"Can I choose a custom finish for the product?"
(Ugh! Your company doesn't offer custom finishes.)
"Can you ship your product in two days for this week's convention?"
(Ugh! A rush order takes five days to assemble and ship.)
"Can you knock 15 percent off the price to match your competitor?"
(Ugh! The competitor is a local, nonunion company with no national overhead costs.)

When a buyer makes a negotiation request that you know you can't fulfill, remain relaxed. Breathe. In fact, take a deep breath right now. As relaxed as you feel reading this book, that's how relaxed you should feel when a buyer makes a negotiation request.

Why is this important? Early in the sales appointment, you verbally and nonverbally established rapport with the buyer. Because you created rapport, you began to trade behaviors. Trading behaviors worked to your advantage when you made your presentation. You sat up to start your presentation. The buyer followed your behavior and also sat up. You leaned forward to demonstrate your product. Your buyer followed your behavior and leaned forward to view the demo.

But if the buyer raises a concern or makes a negotiation request and you become tense…the buyer will follow your lead and become tense. What is the solution to trading unwanted behaviors? Be prepared for negotiation requests and remain relaxed. Remember that a negotiation request means that the sales process is continuing—it hasn't been stopped with a *no*.

b) Clarify the buyer's request

When a buyer makes a negotiation request, salespeople frequently respond to the request rather than discovering the need behind the request. They respond to the symptom rather than discovering the root cause. When you discover the intention behind the request, you may be able to meet the buyer's need by a different avenue that is more advantageous for your company and the buyer.

As a professional, it is your responsibility to make sure you understand the negotiation request, so you can employ your knowledge and experience to provide the best choices available. So before you respond, ask the buyer some clarifying questions:

Buyer: *"Can you include an extra month of on-site training if we buy?"*

Salesperson: *"We certainly want to provide all the training support you need. Why do you think you will require additional training?"*

Buyer: *"I'm not sure if our people can really learn how to use a new system with only one month of training."*

Salesperson: *"So your concern is making sure your people have adequate support after the initial month's training is finished?"*

Buyer: *"Yes."*

Salesperson: *"Okay. What if we provide you with unlimited free phone support for the second month? We could walk your staff through any small questions that may arise after they've been using the new system for a month. Would that give your people the additional support they need and make you more comfortable about moving ahead?"*

By discovering the intention behind the buyer's negotiation request, you may be able to meet that need in a manner less costly to your company.

c) Ask for something in return

When a buyer asks you for a concession, *always* ask for a concession in return. Why is this important? First, what you request from the buyer determines the value of her negotiation request. When she asks for a concession and you just give it to her, then how does she know how valuable it is to you?

- If you lower the amount without asking the buyer to give something in return, could the buyer conclude that you are overcharging her?
- If you include free shipping without asking for something in return, could the buyer conclude that you should have included free shipping in your original offer?

When you ask the buyer to give something in return, you send the message that your concession is worth the value of what they will give you in return (buying immediately, making a larger initial investment, ordering the more expensive model).

Second, your request for something in return tends to slow down the flow of future negotiation requests from the buyer. She must think for several moments whether she is willing to grant your request. Her thoughts are redirected from what she wants from you to what she is able to give you. When the buyer has to give up something of value in order to receive her negotiation request, it encourages her to think twice before making the next negotiation request. It sends the significant message that this is not a one-way negotiation in which the buyer can keep asking, asking, asking for more concessions without consequence. And that's powerful!

Think how differently the conversation in the last chapter would have gone if the salesperson had responded to the buyer's request like this (for comparison, the earlier responses are in parentheses):

Buyer: *"Can you give me a better price?"*

Salesperson: *("Sure. Does 5 percent less sound better to you?")* *"It might be possible with a larger initial investment. How much additional would you be willing to put down?"*

Buyer: *"How about free shipping?"*

Salesperson: *("I can take care of that.")* *"If we can, are you willing to place your order today?"*

Buyer: *"Can you extend the warranty for another year?"*

Salesperson: *("Uh, I'm only allowed to give an extra six-month warranty.")* *"If you purchase today, we may be able to provide a longer warranty at a lower annual investment."*

Buyer: *"Can I put down half now and pay the balance later?"*

Salesperson: *("Okay.")* *"That is not usually an option. However, if you approve the paperwork today, we can accept a split investment with only a 2 percent fee on the balance."*

Buyer: *"What is your very lowest price?"*

Salesperson: (Quotes the absolute lowest price) *"Do you plan to move forward today?"*

Buyer: *"No."*

Salesperson: *"Then let's revisit that question when you are ready to take action."*

Do you see how each answer makes the buyer more hesitant to keep asking for future concessions? To receive the concessions, the buyer had to make an additional investment, take action today, buy a longer warranty, and pay a 2 percent charge! There was no free lunch!

The third reason to always ask for something in return is that the person who asks the questions controls the conversation. You still have to respond to the buyer's negotiation request, but now your response is on your terms rather than the buyer's terms, because you are directing the flow of the conversation.

Always asking for a concession in return is a good habit to develop.

Pick out the negotiation points of greatest value to you and your company, and make them your standard response to concession requests. You will be surprised how often you will get what you ask for in exchange.

d) Offer additional value rather than lower the price

While the previous step is a habit to be formed, this step is a discipline to be practiced. Agreeing with buyers to lower the investment in your product is usually the worst option and should always be the last resort. Why is it better to add value to your offer rather than reduce price?

The first reason is that your company can usually offer the additional value at wholesale. The value your buyer *perceives* on that added value is retail. For example, you can give the buyer a 10 percent discount, or you can give the buyer an extra 10 percent in product that may cost the company only 5 percent in actual cost.

Another reason to offer additional value rather than reduce the amount is that it maintains your pricing structure for future sales to this same client or referred sales. When you get a referral from a buyer who received a rock-bottom price, that will probably be your starting point for all the people that buyer will refer to you. You may be able to increase the amount to referrals with a cost-of-materials increase, but that probably will not match the 10 or 15 percent that you gave away in price reduction to close the initial sale with your buyer.

In that example, if you had offered 10 or 15 percent more value in extra features, you would enjoy two advantages with the referrals from your buyer:

1. Extra features are harder to explain than price. Price is an easy comparison. The buyer says to the people he referred to you, "Hey, I bought some product from ABC Company. I worked a deal for $50 each. Talk to these guys and see if you can work the same deal." Getting a good price is a bragging point for the buyer to tell someone, showing how he got the upper hand during the negotiation.

But features are often specific to each buyer. Your buyer says, "I need two months of extra online support to get my team through our busy season." When you close the sale with your buyer's referral, it is not the referral's busy season, so the referral does not have the exact same needs. The referral may still ask for the free months, but that gives you wiggle room to meet the referral's negotiation request with different negotiation points.

2. It may help you reach higher bonus levels in the amount of income you earn. It's your job to pay attention to the various fee structures around each of your products and their features. First and foremost, those features need to be what's truly best for your

buyer. Just realize that some of those features may also earn you greater fees.

e) A price concession is the last option

You are nearing the end of the negotiation. You have worked through your long list of negotiation points and tried to build a win-win opportunity by holding your price and giving more value. The buyer listened to your offers but did not agree to buy.

Before conceding price, first secure an agreement from the buyer that if the price is lowered, the buyer will take immediate action and buy from you. Notice the word *if*—you have asked a conditional question. You did not agree to lower the price. You did not say it was even possible. This is a trial close question that simply explores a possibility.

By answering in the positive, the buyer provides a strong indication she will buy if you meet that negotiation request. Think that through for a moment. You have not said that you are able to lower the price, but she has told you that if you can, she will buy. That is the type of negotiation that will close sales!

Why is it important for you to secure agreement from the buyer to buy before you lower the amount? If you do not, you could end up in a bid-down situation. The buyer says, "Your bid is at $4,100 and your competitor's bid is at $3,600." You respond by having a conversation about the additional value in your product and services, but regardless, the buyer does not relent. "Match the competitor's price or I will buy from them."

You sense it is an ultimatum, so you go back to your office and beg, plead, and bargain your way down to $3,600. Whew! You e-mail the bid to the buyer the next morning. That afternoon, you call to schedule a time to pick up the approved agreement and a check. "Hey, I'm so excited I was able to talk my manager into matching that competitor's amount," you begin. "It was not an easy conversation. But we got the amount down to where you wanted. What is a good time for me to stop by and take care of the paperwork?" There is a pause. The buyer says, "Well, earlier this afternoon, the competition lowered their price to $3,300."

That's called a bid-down situation. The buyer uses your competition to force you into a lower bid. Then the buyer uses your matching bid to force the competition to reduce their bid. Back and forth it goes, the amount plummeting with each round—probably to zero, if you and the competition are foolish enough to keep playing the bid-down game. And why wouldn't the buyer continue to play the game? The buyer's intention is to get the lowest possible amount she can.

What should you do about bid-down situations? That is a great question to discuss with your sales manager: How much does your company want that particular sale? How much profit is your company willing to concede to get that business? The philosophy of some companies is to make almost any offer. Other companies will accept only sales that meet certain profit guidelines.

If times are slow, sometimes a company will take a loss (as defined by the company accounting department) on a job just to keep people working and to gain a client who will hopefully make additional purchases in the future. So make sure you clearly understand when and why your company wants you to walk away from a sale.

Taking that as a given, if you are selling a *value*-based product against a *price*-based product, trying to compete on price is a recipe for an unfulfilling sales career. When selling value, you can avoid bid-down situations by establishing your value proposition early in the sales appointment with the discovery question about pricing: "Is the lowest price your only consideration, or is quality also important?" You want to hear the buyer say something like "Price is important, but we also want the quality to be good."

If you received a similar answer earlier in the sale, this is a great time to remind buyers of their earlier words. "I'm sorry, I thought you said earlier that you were interested in both pricing and quality."

"Well...yes."

"Do you feel it is reasonable to pay the same for two different levels of quality?"

"Um..."

Remain calm because that earns you more negotiating time with the buyer. Sincerely ask about the buyer's previous statement with the intention to understand. You want to discover what she is thinking at this point. If your buyer suggests your value-based product should be priced the same as your price-based competition, then you probably didn't persuade her very well about the value of your product during the presentation.

The second way to avoid a bid-down situation is to refuse to participate. Let's replay the example above. The buyer says, "Your bid is at $4,100 and your competitor's bid is at $3,600. Match the competitor's price or I will buy from them."

You respond with, "I'll be glad to see what we can do for you about lowering your investment. However, to ensure getting you the highest-quality product, I may not be able to match the competitor's bid."

Many buyers are so conditioned to deal in price, they are caught off guard. "Well, uh...why not?" your buyer asks.

That is your opportunity to affirm the value of your products. "Because there are too many ways to cut corners when the money is tight. We don't believe in cutting corners. We charge enough to do the job right the first time."

You've just planted a seed of insecurity in the buyer's mind. She starts to wonder what she'll lose in quality by playing the price game. You just reset the focus of the conversation from price back to value. If she is still in the conversation, she will probably say, "How low can you go?"

"I'll check on it and get back to you as quickly as possible." What you've just done here is to stall her from purchasing from the competition. If she's really interested in how low you can go, she will wait for your answer before making any decisions.

The buyer may decide that value is a more important factor after all. Or the buyer may go ahead and buy from the competitor. But one thing the buyer won't do is bid down your company and negatively affect your ability to move your product at a higher amount with other potential clients. You opted out of the bid-down situation, protected your margin structure, and made a powerful statement to the buyer about the value of your products. More important, you have made a powerful statement to *yourself* about the value of your products. Most salespeople "talk the talk" about the value of their products, but their actions betray their level of conviction when buyers squeeze them on price.

What if you are not sure about how to respond to a negotiation request?

When buyers make a negotiation request that requires research or permission from your office, the commonsense answer is to let the buyer know that you will check and get back to her as quickly as possible. But in the excitement of a sales call, common sense does not always carry the day. Do not promise something you are not sure you can deliver. Even though it may interrupt the flow of the sales appointment and delay the sale, it is better to move with confidence than to overpromise and recontact the buyer with news that you can't deliver.

WRAPPING UP THE NEGOTIATION

There are several possibilities you may encounter toward the end of a negotiation:

1.   As you are negotiating, the buyer may express another concern or question.

> "So tell me again why your new system is better."
> "I'm still not convinced you can deliver it in time."
> "My owner prefers the competitor's equipment."

That takes your conversation back to the inner circle. That's okay. The persuasion process flows back and forth between negotiation and addressing questions and concerns. Because you now know how to recognize both, you are able to respond accordingly.

2.   When you have covered all of your possible negotiation points and the customer *still* won't budge, how do you respond? Ask the ultimate question: "We've been discussing many possibilities during our time together. What would need to happen for you to take action today?" After you ask this question, remain relaxed and...wait. Don't say a word until the buyer speaks. Whether it is five minutes or an hour, remain silent. If the quiet time is long enough, be prepared for the buyer to act like he forgot the question.

> "Are we done?"
> "I'm sorry to repeat myself, but I asked you what would need to happen for you to take action today."

Again remain silent. Remember, there are three basic activities in selling: making statements, asking questions, and remaining silent. After you ask the buyer to take action, remain silent until the buyer speaks again. Silence is simple...but it's also powerful.

3.   Deliver a summary. When all else has been discussed, including the ultimate question, and it is time to walk, concisely state your case. And finish with something like this: "My company is all about delivering quality. If you want the benefits of the value that is built into our products, then this is the amount."

Say it kindly but say it firmly. And even if you don't get the sale, you will walk away from the sales appointment knowing that you explored every possibility in a professional manner. If you think the buyer will choose a price-driven company that does not offer quality products or services, then make a note in your calendar to follow up in a few weeks. The buyer will appreciate your follow-up. Occasionally, if the price-based company has dropped the ball, the buyer will look to your company to get him back on track.

Scenario 1: Business Sales Appointment

Long before the sales appointment began, Kate had listed her negotiation points in preparation for all her appointments with potential clients:

- extend warranty
- extend online customer support
- include two overtime service calls each year
- break payments into thirds
- free annual widget tests
- eliminate administration closing fees
- customized colors when the client pays cash
- free shipping
- express shipping

Kate typically offers these negotiation points on the condition that a potential client will make an immediate buying decision.

During their journey around the inner circle, Kate discovered Mr. Stevens's concerns, and she got his agreement that if she could respond satisfactorily to his concerns, then nothing else would prevent him from taking action today. Then she responded to each of his concerns, confirmed that he was satisfied, and once again asked him to say *yes*.

Mr. Stevens furrows his brow and stares at the ceiling. "If I buy more than one widget, what type of discount would I get?"

Kate replies, "How many were you thinking of?"

"I've got three teams that could benefit from a more reliable widget. What could you do if I bought three widgets?"

"The investment would remain the same, but I may be able to get permission from my office to extend your warranty for those three widgets by six months. They would probably consider that extension if you are planning to move forward today."

Kate senses that he has some other topics he wants to discuss, so she does not lead him to the next moment of decision...yet. "What else should we talk about?"

He considers her question. "Extra support would be helpful. It takes a while for some of these guys to get used to the features of a newer widget..." Suddenly he changes subjects. "Why does everyone charge so much for widget annual inspections?"

Kate grimaces in empathy. "You know better than anyone the challenges that can be caused by widgets that don't perform properly."

"All too well, unfortunately. But really, $500 per widget for an annual inspection? You guys are killing me."

"Complying with government regulations can be costly," Kate agrees.

Mr. Stevens frowns. He expected her to push back on his verbal jab and justify Widget Corp's pricing of inspections. He gives her a few moments to offer lowering the price but she simply looks at him in silence. He continues, "What can you do on the pricing of your annual inspections?"

"Dean, I have a lot more leverage in asking my office to authorize requests when I know that you are ready to move forward today."

He weighs her words. "I am thinking about a couple of widgets."

"Before, you mentioned three," Kate says without emotion.

Realizing how closely she is listening to his words, Mr. Stevens speaks more deliberately. "If I bought three widgets, would you include the annual inspections for free with the service contract?"

Earlier in the sales appointment, when Kate learned how many teams Mr. Stevens had in the field, her goal became to enroll *every* team's widget on a Widget Corp service agreement. She shifts the conversation in that direction. "Currently, you have six teams in the field using widgets. If you upgrade your three unreliable widgets and give us the service agreement on all of your remaining widgets, then my company will be more inclined to include the annual inspections."

Mr. Stevens shrugs. "I am not opposed to that. We're on a month-to-month contract because I am not happy with their service. So you are saying you will give me free annual inspections on all six widgets?"

"If you move forward on the investment in three new widgets and give us the service agreement on all your remaining widgets." She uses the phrase "all your remaining widgets" because she is not certain how many widgets he plans to own in the near future. Whatever the number, she wants the service agreement on *every* widget.

A few moments of silence pass as Mr. Stevens considers the savings. Kate keeps her body relaxed and remains ready to respond to Mr. Stevens's reply.

His eyes narrow as he gives his next negotiation request. "But we still have the monthly service fee to work out. You charge $80 a month per widget *more* than our current provider. Multiply that times six teams...that's $480 a month. That's too much."

Kate could remind him of the delays his teams experienced with their current widgets that cost him thousands of dollars in billing time. However, she believes that would take the conversation *farther* from the next closing moment rather than *nearer* to it. Instead, she chooses to remind him that they are now closer to an agreement than before. "If we provide free annual inspections on each of your widgets, that $500 savings divided by twelve months would equate to over $40 a month in value per widget. That brings us within $40 of your current provider."

Mr. Stevens nods in agreement. Kate believes she is closing in on getting a *yes*, so she presses on. "How much do you pay monthly for phone support with your current service provider?"

Mr. Stevens picks up the competitor's service agreement and starts glancing through the pricing section. Kate knows the pricing is *not* in the agreement but allows Mr. Stevens to discover that for himself. "Ah, that's right. Our local widget company doesn't provide phone support," he explains to Kate as he phones his assistant for the pricing. "As you probably know, it's provided directly by the manufacturer."

Kate most certainly knows that. And she knows how much the manufacturer charges for their phone support.

Mr. Stevens's assistant gives him the answer. "What? I thought it was $15 a month. When did they raise it?"

Kate suppresses a smile. The manufacturer raised the cost of their monthly phone support four months earlier. She heard similar reactions from other potential clients on several occasions.

Mr. Stevens sets the phone down. "We pay $25 a month for phone support."

Kate gives him a few moments for the math to sink in before she continues. "Because we manufacture our widgets in-house instead of depending on a third-party manufacturer, our phone support is included in our monthly investment. So really, with the $40 saved in annual inspections and the $25 a month you will save in not paying for third-party phone support, we are really only $15 above your current provider."

She can see that Mr. Stevens is beginning to waver, but his mind is still churning.

Mr. Stevens looks down at the Widget Corp image on her tablet and weighs the value she has presented during their appointment. He hates the idea of paying more each month in service fees, but he hates the delays and costs of widget downtime even more. He decides that if he is going to pay more in monthly service fees, he wants to get a final bit of additional value. "Get me down to the same price as my current provider, and I'll make the switch."

Again, Kate suppresses a smile. Mr. Stevens is finally ready to reach an agreement. She mentally reviews her list of negotiation points. Based on what he said earlier, she chooses her negotiation point to close the gap. "How many overtime service calls did you have last year?"

"Hmm. I'd have to research that. Usually our guys work 8:00 a.m. to 4:00 p.m., but sometimes incoming weather demands that we finish the job that day, so we'll work into the evening." He chuckles. "Of course, whenever a team is working overtime, their widget always breaks down at 4:01 p.m., when overtime service calls begin."

Kate smiles at his joke. It is a brief break in the tension of decision making.

Mr. Stevens continues, "I don't know. Maybe a half dozen times a year."

"So about one overtime call each year per widget? How much do you pay in overtime service calls?"

"Now you are asking some painful questions," he says, half joking. "Something like $285 an hour."

"With a minimum two-hour charge?"

"That sounds right. Geez, you're ruining my day," he adds drily.

She smiles again and continues. "So each overtime call, at a minimum of two hours, costs at least $570. Multiply $570 times six overtime calls a year, and you are paying several thousand dollars in overtime costs."

She waits for his agreement, which he finally gives with a nod of his head.

"Earlier, you said that if I work with you on the $15 per month difference in service fees, then you would be ready to move forward today."

He nods again.

"The remaining difference of $15 a month times six widgets is $90 a month. Multiply that times twelve months..." She takes out a written agreement from her bag and turns it over. Using a pencil, she does the calculation on the back of the Widget Corp agreement so he can see the math. "That comes to $1,080 a year. Are we agreed on that amount?"

"Yes."

Kate begins her close. "If you agree to three new widgets today and enroll all of your widgets on our service agreement, then my office can authorize three free overtime calls per year on any of your widgets. That includes the widgets you purchase from us and any of your existing widgets that you continue to use."

She turns the written agreement over, and in the Special Conditions section she neatly prints, *Three free overtime calls per year with the purchase of three new widgets from Widget Corp.* As she writes, she says, "That's over $1,500 of value, and it more than covers the $15 a month per widget that you requested."

She turns the written agreement around so he can read it, but she deliberately does not push the written agreement in his direction. "Is that what we agreed?"

Kate sits back in her seat and remains relaxed. Mr. Stevens looks at her handwritten notes and says nothing. Then he reaches over and picks up the agreement. Turning to page one, he begins glancing through the paragraphs until he returns to her notes in the Special Conditions section.

"So phone support is included," he says. "You will give me free annual inspections. And you'll give me three free overtime calls per year. Can I have six overtime calls, one for each widget?"

Kate appeals to his character and being a man of his word. "You asked me to work with you on the remaining $15 per month to reach an agreement. I've exceeded that. Is this what we agreed?"

He thinks for several moments and makes his final decision. "Well, we are ready for some better service for our widgets. What do you and I need to do?"

"If you would please get me the registration numbers on your current widgets, I'll fill out the rest of the information for your authorization on the written agreement." She looks at the written agreement in his hands as she speaks.

Taking her nonverbal cue, he hands her the agreement and picks up the phone to call his assistant for the registration numbers.

Kate quickly fills in the service agreement for all of Mr. Stevens's widgets as well as the written order for the three new widgets. Her expression is pleasant as she fills in the written agreement, but her thoughts remain focused. She is successfully closing *this* sale, but she has one more task to complete to pave the way for future sales...

Scenario 2: Residential Sales Appointment

Bob's pre-prepared written list of negotiation points looks like this:

- pay 10 percent deposit now, the rest on delivery
- free upgrades with cash
- company financing plan
- customized features allow control of final amount
- qualifying for tax credit
- free delivery
- purchase extra warranty
- cap on annual premium increases
- can pass services to heirs
- preferred members service line

Bob has journeyed around the inner circle with Pat and Gary. He confirmed that learning how to use widgets and cash flow were the only reasons they were not ready to take immediate action. They agreed that if he adequately addressed those concerns, they would take action today.

After presenting the option to pay in three installments, Bob asks them to take action.

Then Gary asks, "Can we have sixty days between payments instead of thirty days?"

Instead of immediately responding to Gary's negotiation request, Bob decides to find out more about Gary's intention for his negotiation request. "Let's talk about that. What is your concern about making a payment every thirty days?"

"My busy season begins in March, but with our billing cycle, the payments we receive from clients don't start coming in until early May."

Bob considers his words. "You are concerned you won't have the funds available to make a payment every thirty days?"

Gary grimaces. "Well, we have the funds, but I am not comfortable with cutting things too close during the slow season."

Bob nods. Earlier in the appointment, Bob asked Gary and Pat if they had the funds available to make a buying decision. Gary seemingly indicated that they did, and he confirmed it again just now. The question is whether Gary wants to tap into his available funds. Bob wants to clarify the nature of Gary's cash flow concerns. "Is your concern about a temporary cash flow situation this month or the availability of the funds in the coming months?"

"This month is particularly tight, but until my busy season starts, we like to make sure we have enough on hand to pay the bills."

Bob is about to speak when Pat asks, "How much is the service policy?"

Bob gives her the monthly amount.

Pat continues, "We're going to have this for many years. How much will the service policy be, for example, ten years from now?"

Bob points to the terms in the written agreement. "Depending on the rate of inflation in the market index of the basic materials, it can increase up to 4 percent a year during the course of your five-year service policy."

"Four percent?" Pat does the math in her head. "That could be up to 20 percent in five years!"

Bob replies without emotion, "If the price index of basic materials rises, then that is possible. We would simply be passing on the materials increase."

Pat murmurs disapprovingly. "That seems like a lot."

"If that rate of inflation occurs in the materials index, it could be a lot," Bob agrees. He believes that trying to convince her that 4 percent is *not* a lot would take her and Gary farther from the next moment of decision rather than nearer to it. He acknowledged her emotions and waits for her response.

"Um…" Pat furrows her brow, not sure what to say next. She expected him to tell her a 4 percent annual increase was not a big deal. "I mean, can you do anything about that?"

"Sure," Bob replies casually. "If you agree to a ten-year service agreement, we can authorize a 2 percent cap adjustment on the service agreement. That means the cost of your service policy can't be increased more than 2 percent each year for the next ten years."

Pat nods in approval. Gary adds, "I'm fine with that. But I still don't think I am ready to move forward now."

Gary looks at Pat, whose expression has clouded. "Sixty-six hundred dollars this month for Diane's program! Then there is the airline ticket. And then at least two months until regular income from the busy season. Maybe we can do this later this spring."

Pat looks resignedly at Bob and says nothing. Gary turns to Bob. "We really like your product. And we do want to buy a widget. It's just not good timing for us right now."

Bob consciously relaxes his body as he listens to Gary. It seemed like they were moving closer to the next moment of decision, but now they're stuck again on cash flow. Bob has explored the cash flow issue from several angles, and there are only two arrows left in his quiver to move Gary and Pat to the next moment of decision. The first is to define their basic options.

"Look, this is a long-term decision," Bob begins. "The important thing this evening is making the best decision for both of you. So let's summarize what we've discussed tonight. You basically have three choices. The first choice is to decide not to invest in a widget at all. Earlier this evening, we talked about the difficulties that may cause in the future for your family." Normally Bob uses the word *challenges*, but to emphasize his point, he uses the word *difficulties*.

Bob continues, "The second choice is to take the next step today to invest in your widget. You have said on several occasions how your family will benefit from that."

They both nod.

"And you've expressed your appreciation for the features of the Residential Widget."

Again they nod.

Bob sighs. "The third choice is to simply put off the decision. The advantage is that you will have extra cash on hand through your slow season. The disadvantage is that you are both busy people. Behind the upcoming bills for Diane's trip are more bills. There are always more bills. There are always more reasons to put off getting a widget. That is why over 60 percent of families face the difficulties of getting caught without a widget. And when that time comes when your family needs your widget the most... all the temporary reasons that distracted you from getting your widget will seem inconsequential."

Bob gives Pat and Gary a few moments to absorb the three choices. They have reached the next moment of decision, and Bob is prepared to patiently wait for their response. Gary slowly shakes his head. "I don't want to spend the money with Diane's trip coming due. This is just a bad time."

Bob allows a few seconds of silence to pass. Lowering his voice a bit, he employs the final arrow in his quiver by asking them the ultimate question. "You've said on several occasions that you are sold on the value of owning a widget." He pauses as they both nod in agreement. "So what would need to happen for you to move forward *today* on getting your widget?"

Bob asked that question with an authentic concern to discover a transaction that works for them. With that state's three-day right of rescission regulation, he knows that pressing Pat and Gary into a sale they really don't believe in would most probably end with a cancelled order. Pat and Gary have bought into the value of owning a widget. They have access to the funds to purchase a widget. What Bob is helping them with is the emotional process of making a decision. Pat seems to have made her decision. Gary is having a challenge making his decision.

Bob sits back in his chair waiting for their response. The

pleasant expression on his face reflects his satisfaction in leading Pat and Gary through the entire Circle of Persuasion.

Sometimes, couples at this point in the sales appointment respond with a solution allowing them to say *yes*. But many times, couples say *no*. If Pat and Gary's answer is *no*, Bob will arrange a time to follow up. Because of their positive response to his product, he will also ask for referrals before he leaves their home that evening.

Gary is looking down at his hands. "I don't think we should do it."

Pat asks, "What if we borrowed from the trust account?"

Gary looks up. "What?"

"The kids' trust account. Why don't we borrow this first payment from their trust account? We are allowed to borrow once a year on their behalf. After all, they will ultimately benefit the most from the widget. We'll make the second payment. The third payment won't be due until after the busy season begins. We'll pay back the trust account this summer."

Gary considers her suggestion. "That could work." He looks at Bob. "Do you accept personal checks?"

"Personal checks and major credit cards," Bob replies.

Pat adds, "If we use our credit card, we can get airline points."

Gary thinks for several moments and picks up the sales agreement. "We'll make the first payment from the trust account...but thirty days from now is too soon for us to make the second payment. Can you make it forty-five days?"

They have returned to Gary's original negotiation request. Bob has some flexibility in this area, and his negotiation point is getting Gary's agreement for immediate action.

"If you move forward today with the written agreement, I will get permission from the office to deliver your widget in forty-five days rather than thirty. That will allow you to move the second investment back fifteen days. Does that make it easier for you to move forward?"

Gary looks at Pat, who is smiling. She says, "Okay. Let's do that."

"If you have the credit card handy, I'll finish preparing the agreement," Bob says, nodding at the written agreement in Gary's hands.

Gary hands Bob the written agreement and reaches for his wallet. As Bob asks Pat to confirm the shipping details, he focuses on filling in the agreement correctly. But he knows one last task lies ahead...

CHAPTER 16 KEY POINTS

- Remain relaxed when the buyer makes a negotiation request.
- Always discover the intention of the buyer's request before responding.
- Keep control of the negotiation by asking for a concession in return for what you are offering.
- Always offer more value before offering to lower the amount.
- As a last resort, always get agreement from the buyer to take immediate action before you agree to reduce the amount.
- To avoid bid-down situations on value-based products, let the buyer know you will work on reducing the amount, but you will not match the competitor's price.
- Negotiations can quickly switch back to addressing concerns. Be ready for both.
- If your negotiation ends without agreement, always ask the ultimate question.

SECTION 4

—

The Buyer Said Yes

17. When Buyers Say Yes!

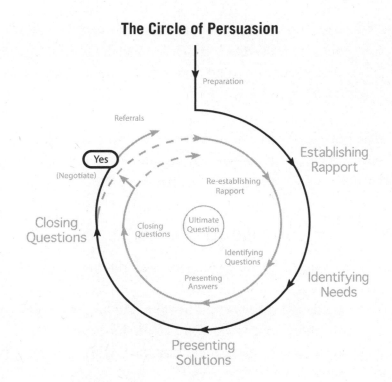

The Circle of Persuasion

Preparation

Referrals

Yes

(Negotiate)

Establishing Rapport

Re-establishing Rapport

Closing Questions

Closing Questions

Ultimate Question

Identifying Questions

Presenting Answers

Identifying Needs

Presenting Solutions

The buyer says *yes*!

   Ah...the feeling of satisfaction when you realize your efforts have been rewarded with a positive response from your buyer. Buyers say *yes* in many ways:

1. The buyer directly says that she will buy.

"Yes, I'll buy it."
"Okay. Write it up."
"I'll take three."

2. Or, she indirectly says she will buy by asking confirmation questions that presuppose the sale.

"So you will have the product to me by Friday?"
"So I can use my credit card to purchase the product?"
"So you're going to extend my online support for a year if I pay cash?"

3. The buyer nonverbally indicates she will buy with a nod of the head or a deep sigh as she relaxes and sits back in her chair. She reaches for a pen to approve the paperwork.

YOU DID YOUR JOB WELL

- You demonstrated real conviction about the value of your product.
- You established rapport and became the kind of likable person with whom your buyer wants to do business.
- You identified her needs, including the buying dynamics that allow her to buy today.
- Your presentation was geared to her specific needs.
- You asked for her business in a compelling manner.
- You remained relaxed and silent until she responded.
- You competently journeyed around the inner circle and brought her back to a moment of decision.

And now... she's said *yes*.

How do you respond when a buyer says *yes*? Do you jump up and down, pump your fist, whoop and holler, and set off fireworks? "Really? You mean it? Gosh-golly! That's great. I mean, uh... let's see. Paperwork. Hmm. Let's start with..."

That's a bit of dramatization—but ask yourself, do you nonverbally show surprise? Do your eyes get big with astonishment? Does an uncontrollable smile break out on your face, as if you'd just gotten asked to the big dance by the most popular kid in school? Or do you calmly begin attending to the buying details with quiet expectation?

When the buyer says *yes*, be sure to remain warm and friendly and calm. Affirm your pleasure in a professional manner. A slight nod of your head in acknowledgment is fine. A pleasant expression of appreciation is good. A quick verbal affirmation—"Fantastic"— simply spoken, with the calm expectation that you appreciate her business and her decisiveness in making an educated buying decision.

Many average-performing salespeople picture themselves giving presentations and answering questions, but they don't think beyond the moment when the buyer says *yes*. But how you respond after the buyer says *yes* has profound implications for your future business with her and anyone she may refer to you.

After the buying decision has been made, you may notice that the buyer visibly relaxes. The anxiety of decision making subsides, and a mental shift occurs as the buyer begins seeing you as her consultant and service provider rather than as a salesperson. It is to your advantage to make the same kind of psychological shift.

Also, notice that you are seeing another shift in the ebb and flow of rapport. Early in the sales appointment, you established rapport and maintained it through the presentation. When you asked your closing questions in the outer circle, rapport may have been temporarily affected. When you began your journey around the inner circle, you quickly re-established rapport and maintained it through addressing the buyer's questions and concerns. When you closed the second time, rapport may have been affected at the next moment of decision.

Now that the buyer has said *yes*, it is time to re-establish rapport once again as you take care of the buying details. Your tone continues to be friendly. Your facial expressions are more relaxed. As you work through the buying details, you've now assumed the role of trusted advisor.

Your next step is to verify the accuracy of all the information related to the sale. You will outline what happens next for the buyer as your new client, such as:

- how the buyer can expect to be treated,
- how to reach you and your customer service or support department with any questions that arise,
- when you'll next be in touch with the buyer, and
- how often you'll be in contact with the buyer to assure she remains satisfied with her decision.

Making the initial sale is a process. But keeping clients satisfied is a process as well, and just as important.

Attending to the details of the sale is largely industry specific, but here are a few principles to consider.

AFTER-THE-SALE PRINCIPLES

1. *Time.* If, by this point in the sales appointment, the buyer is running short on time, use your judgment to determine which key buying details have the highest priority. For example, getting authorization and payment may be relatively quick, but writing up specific details of the product or filling out the paperwork for ship-

ping addresses and times of delivery may take longer. Determine if other employees—such as an assistant in the buyer's office—can help with nonessential details. Perhaps that option might be wise to suggest to the buyer after you've received the authorization.

Note: When completing the nonessential buying details after a buyer says *yes*, the buyer's time should be given extra priority. If in doubt, simply ask, "Jim, getting the rest of the information required to arrange delivery of your order will take about another fifteen minutes. Do you have the time, or should I meet with your assistant about these last few details?"

---

2. *Receiving the investments.* Be careful about reaching over too quickly and taking the buyer's cash, check, or credit card. There is a fine line between buyers giving you the money and you taking it from them.

For example, you are sitting across from a buyer who approves the agreement, writes a check, and then leaves the check and agreement on the table where she signed it. It's usually best to not reach across the table, take the agreement and check, and pull them back toward you. It is better to err on the side of caution and let the money remain on the table until the buyer actually gives it to you.

Most buyers will not place significant importance on this detail. However, you may encounter a few who do place importance on your actions at this point. Always err on the side of caution. After all the work that you've done to get the sale, you don't want to risk a small detail like this distracting buyers from the relieved feelings of making a wise buying decision. Do nothing that could cause them to question your sincerity in serving their needs.

3. *Organized paperwork.* One subtle thing that reveals your level of expectancy and your professionalism is how organized you are with your paperwork. If the buyer says *yes* and you start rifling through your pockets and notebook looking for a pen, that might communicate that you are disorganized. If you have to run to your car to get a written agreement, that does not reflect well on your expectancy for this presentation or your professionalism. Before you begin the sales appointment, invest thirty seconds in checking all of your necessary closing materials. Mentally picturing the appointment from start to finish will help you make note of what you need at hand to be most prepared.

4. *Be prepared for buying questions.* Another aspect of organization is familiarizing yourself with the answers to questions frequently asked after the buying decision has been made. If you don't know the answers to questions about basic features, delivery options, or financing options, that will not reflect well on you. The occasional questions about odd details may require research, but buyers will expect you to be prepared for questions that are frequently asked by existing clients.

Okay, let's assume the basic buying details have been settled. You've received the necessary authorization and investment. The paperwork has been completed. You are finished, right? Pack your bags and head out the door to your next sales appointment.

Not so fast. You've done a great job in getting this sale, and that is cause for celebration. There will be plenty of time for that celebration later. But right now, don't walk away from the opportunity to multiply your sales efforts. You have one more task to complete that will make future journeys around the Circle of Persuasion much easier and much quicker. We'll cover that in the next chapter.

CHAPTER 17 KEY POINTS

- Buyers may say *yes* directly, indirectly, or with a simple nod.
- Remain warm and friendly while completing the sale.
- Verify the accuracy of all the necessary information.
- Continue to be aware of any time constraints on the buyer.
- Wait for the buyer to directly hand you the approved paperwork and investment.
- Tell your new client how she can expect to have her needs served.

18.

Earning the Right to Even More Yeses

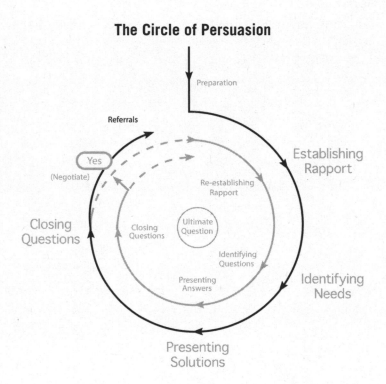

The Circle of Persuasion

Preparation

Referrals

Yes

(Negotiate)

Re-establishing Rapport

Establishing Rapport

Closing Questions

Closing Questions

Ultimate Question

Identifying Questions

Presenting Answers

Identifying Needs

Closing Questions

Presenting Solutions

Y ou began this sales process by selling the buyer on meeting with you. You used your well-honed sales skills to work your way around the Circle of Persuasion. You've demonstrated a high degree of professionalism. Therefore, you've earned the right to gain more than just this one sale from your new client. Your relationship should be comfortable enough at this point that you can confidently ask for referrals or quality introductions.

Here's the truth: people who are referred to you are much more likely to buy. That's because the person doing the referring is usually a liked and trusted associate or relative. If you haven't done so already, incorporate the step of asking for referrals into every client contact you make. Doing so will practically guarantee you a successful career.

Average salespeople won't take this step. Why? Anxiety about asking buyers for too much keeps salespeople from getting referred leads from new clients. You just asked them to buy. You asked them to fill out a written agreement to settle buying details. Now you are asking them for something again! Geez, when does all this asking stop?

The underlying cause of the above anxiety is found in our discussion in chapter 5 about whether the buyer's *no* started with you. Your level of conviction about the value of your products and services becomes apparent this one last time in the sales process.

- How do you feel about asking someone to buy? Are you asking them to do something for *you*?
- How do you feel about settling the details for the sale and the paperwork? Are you fearful that buyers will change their minds?
- How do you feel about asking buyers for referrals? Do you feel like you're imposing on them?

Take a moment and turn this perspective around. Look at referrals from your satisfied buyer's point of view. He has been seeking solutions to some challenges. He received an effective, value-based solution that makes his life more productive and enjoyable. People love to tell their friends and coworkers when they find a great solution. And he found a great solution at a fair amount with you, right?

You have established something new in common with your buyer. You both have the desire to help others benefit from the solution to the same challenge. Your buyer is now going to tell others about the solution to his challenges, anyway. Why not also have the buyer tell about the person who brought him the solution? You!

SETTING UP THE REFERRAL

A thriving referral business doesn't happen by accident. Below are several suggestions for setting up an effective request for referrals.

Exceptional buying experience

This may seem obvious, but the best way to set up asking for referrals is by providing an exceptional buying experience. That means the buyer enjoys your level of professionalism and the quality of your product.

It is important to note that delivering an exceptional buying experience alone will not automatically bring you referrals. You must still ask for them.

Wait-and-see salespeople, as they do with most parts of the sales appointment, make getting referrals a separate part of the sale. On occasions when they close a sale, they turn to the buyer and say, "One last thing. Who else do you know who would be interested in this product?"

It is the first mention of referrals in the entire sales appointment. Does it work? Sometimes, because anything works occasionally, but for most people it's too abrupt. That reflects on the power of asking, not the effectiveness of springing a request for referrals upon buyers without warning. The question is whether that strategy is the most productive and the most enjoyable way to ask for referrals. The answer is no.

A frequent theme of the Circle of Persuasion is to approach sales like a game of chess. Intentionally use your actions early in the sales appointment to achieve your objectives later in the sales appointment. Setting up the referral follows this same strategy. Throughout the sales process, appropriately mention referrals so that the buyer learns early on that providing referrals is an expected part of their buying experience.

But how you can introduce the idea of referrals in a natural manner?

The process of getting referrals or introductions to qualified potential clients begins the moment you meet people. You must be like a detective and look for clues as to the small groups of people they know. And as noted, the right to ask for the introductions should be set up in the very beginning **and continue throughout the sales process**. Here are some ways to do this:

1. When introducing your company: "John, you may not have seen a tremendous amount of advertising about our company. We have chosen to focus on building our business primarily by word-of-mouth recommendations from satisfied clients. So when we have done the job, and you are happy with our company and the benefits of our product and service, you wouldn't have any reservations about providing me with introductions to a few other people you know with similar needs to yours, would you?"

2. When describing the level of service your company offers: "Our objective is to provide such exceptional service that you can't wait to refer us to your colleagues."

3. When telling a story or giving a testimonial: "A client referred me to Sheila, an office manager who said her company had a challenge with..."

When you say a word, then the buyer must mentally process it. When you mention referrals several times during the sales appointment, you are directing his mind to process the idea of referrals and foreshadowing your future request for his referrals.

RAPPORT AND REFERRALS

One last time, we return to the importance of having well-established rapport throughout the sales process. We are now past the point of decision. The tension of making a decision is gone. Physically, you may not move an inch, but in your thoughts, words, and actions, you make an important shift in your business relationship. Your words and your nonverbal communications that reinforce this mental shift help take the buyer farther away from the moment of decision and farther into your relationship as his provider.

How can you nonverbally support that shift? As you pleasantly yet efficiently wrap up the details of the sale, use your tonality and physiology to return the buyer to the relaxed, rapport-building atmosphere you created before the presentation began. If the buyer asks postsale questions about using your products and services, answer them and encourage other questions. Not appearing eager to leave communicates confidence in your belief that the buyer made the right decision.

ASKING FOR REFERRALS AT THE CLOSE

As we examine the details of the process of asking for referrals, we will look at two scenarios. The first is asking for a referral at the end of your presentation. This would be done in a conversational manner just like the rest of your sales presentation. Follow these steps to complete an effective request for referrals:

Step #1: Isolate faces for the buyer to see. Bring up small groups of people she knows. You have paid attention and made notes during your conversation with your buyer. Some of what you noted included any groups or organizations the buyer participates in. With consumer sales, you would note the mention of any friends or family members.

Start your referral request like this: "Mary, you mentioned that you participate in a networking group. When you think about your fellow members, who comes to mind as having similar needs as those you expressed here today?"

Step #2: Capture those names. Ideally, you would jot them on a notepad. Jumping to entering them into your contact database is a bit brusque.

Step #3: Ask qualifying questions: "What was it they said or did that brought them to mind just now?" Note the buyer's answers. This is great information that will provide you with conversation starters when you contact the referrals.

Step #4: Ask for contact information: "What's the best way for me to reach them?" If the client doesn't have contact information at hand, remain patient and suggest where she might find it: "If you spoke recently, perhaps you have his number in your phone." This is an especially good suggestion to make, because while she's scrolling through her phone list, she might come upon someone else who would be a good candidate for your product.

Step #5: Ask her to call and introduce you. Don't balk at this. There is a very good reason to make this request. "Since you're so happy with the benefits our product will be providing your company, would you mind making a quick call to let Jonathan know that you have found a solution that might help him as well?" Few people will feel comfortable making that type of call. That's okay, because you're going to relieve any discomfort this question creates.

Step #6: If the buyer shows nervousness, ask for permission just to use her name. Most buyers will be so relieved to be off the hook on making that call that they will jump at this step. Once they agree, promise them you will do your part: "Mary, because you have asked me to reach out to Jonathan, I promise I will contact him and give him the highest-quality service possible. May I have your permission to use your name when I contact him by mail [or in person]?"

ASKING FOR REFERRALS LATER IN THE RELATIONSHIP

The second scenario is asking for referrals during the course of your ongoing business relationship. When is the best time to ask for a referral? Any time you deliver outstanding service to your client, it is a great time to ask him for referrals. Another time is when you help a client resolve a challenge. When clients are happy, confirm the value that you bring to them and remind them that you appreciate their referrals.

The process will look something like this:

A. Make a list of your top satisfied clients. Call or see them just after you do something for them that they really appreciate.
B. During your conversation, ask them to affirm that they value your service. For example, "How did the [service you performed or problem you solved] help you?" Or, "Are you happy with the service we provided for you?"

Most of your top clients will be delighted with your products and services. When they express their satisfaction, continue with the next step in the referral process.

Note: If they are dissatisfied, STOP the referral process and immediately address their challenges! It makes no sense to ask for a referral if they are unhappy with some aspect of your company's product or service. More important, this is an opportunity to demonstrate excellence in service.

An unhappy client is certainly not your first choice, but consider the opportunity. At no time during your business relationship will you have a better opportunity to show your clients that you are truly their advocate for quality service than when there is a challenge. Talk is cheap when all is going well. It is your actions when service is not at optimal levels that demonstrates to your clients that you do provide exceptional service.

After the storm, you will be pleasantly surprised how many clients will reward you with loyalty and referrals. Days or weeks later, when the situation has been fully resolved to the client's satisfaction, begin this process again.

C. Affirm that you value the client as a customer. "You are a valued customer. We truly appreciate your business!"
D. Remind the client that referrals are an important part of your business. "As you know, a big part of my business is primarily built on referrals from satisfied clients like yourself."

Note: If your clients are business owners themselves, do your best to bring them referred leads as well.

E. Ask for those referrals. "Who else do you know who wrestles with challenges similar to those that we helped you with?"

When you affirm the experience of helping the buyer with his challenges, you provide a reason to ask for his referrals. You are not asking them to give you more business. You are simply asking them for names of people who face similar challenges. That shifts the focus of the benefit from you to your buyer's friends and associates. Clients are emotionally attached to that challenge. The relief of finding a real solution is a powerful emotional incentive to offer possible relief to others.

Let's bring the last few steps together so you can see it at a glance.

"Did the [service you performed or problem you solved] bring value to you? [Yes.] Fantastic! We appreciate your business and consider you one of our top clients. As you know, my business is primarily built on referrals from satisfied clients like yourself. Who else do you know who wrestles with similar challenges that [your actions that day] would solve?"

This statement, like your closing calls to action, needs to be written out in your words and practiced out loud until it becomes second nature. Clients respond better to confident requests. Like with your closing questions, any hesitation in your wording while you are asking for referrals can be interpreted by a buyer as a lack of conviction. The reality is that this is the logical next step of action. You have provided the buyer with value, and your buyers like sharing value-filled opportunities with others.

F. Listen!

Do not interrupt clients when they are thinking of the names of their referrals. Allow them a few moments of thought. In some ways, this is like remaining quiet after the close. The same rule applies. The first one who speaks...well, if you speak first, you may not get any referrals.

Why would salespeople interrupt buyers who are about to give them the names of some valuable referrals? One reason could be the same uncomfortable silence that salespeople experience at the close. Another reason could be a fear that clients won't give them any names.

If you follow the steps above and are careful with the wording you use to ask for referrals, very few clients will say no. The buyer may not give you names right away, saying he wants to think about it or that he will get back to you. While procrastination is not your first desired outcome, it is still a win for you because you have introduced the idea of referrals into the buyer's thoughts, and he has now verbalized his willingness to consider giving names to you.

One way to kick-start the process is to ask about people that the buyer mentioned during the sales appointment. Do you remember all the questions you asked when establishing rapport and identifying his needs? Sometimes during that small talk, buyers will mention names of colleagues and former employees who now work for other companies. Do you remember how taking occasional notes during that time showed that you were listening? Well, if your notes include the names of colleagues and former employees who now work at other companies...then you have potential referrals you can ask about by name. "You mentioned John works at ABC Company now. Would he know who makes the purchasing decision on this type of product?"

When a client begins giving you the names of his referrals, encourage him to give you more names by your nonverbal actions.

1. Write down the names he provides. That shows you are listening. And it helps you remember the names of the referrals later.

2. Do not interrupt your client with questions. If you are not sure of the spelling of a name, jot down your best guess and keep listening. As long as your client continues giving names, continue to remain silent.

3. Give your client some nonverbal encouragement. Once you begin writing, keep looking at your paper with the expectancy of writing more names until the client finally stops. Slowly nod your

head in encouragement at the mention of each name. Remain relaxed and maintain a pleasant expression as he gives you names.

4. Don't ask for the contact information on each name until he finishes talking. Once the client stops giving you names, you can ask about spelling and contact information. If by this point in the sales appointment he is running short on time, ask if the client's assistant could give you the contact information.

G. If possible, contact the referrals the client provides *that same day*. There are several advantages for taking immediate action.

- The names are fresh to you, and your excitement will be at a peak.
- If the referral contacts the client about your call, your client will be more likely to remember your conversation. But if you wait two weeks or a month to call…who knows how much your client will remember?
- Contacting them immediately lets you follow up with your client more quickly.

H. Let your client know the outcome of your contacting his referrals. In general, people like to be helpful. If you help a friend or associate of his resolve a challenge, the client doing the referring will feel like a hero and be very inclined to give you other names.

Be sure to send the referrer a thank-you e-mail or handwritten note after he gives you the leads. Then, send another message after you have contacted his friends and associates. Letting your client know what happened shows that he did not waste his time giving you referrals whom you didn't follow up with. That encourages him to give you more referrals. This is especially true when some of the first batch of referrals also become your satisfied clients.

I. Call your clients regularly to provide service and to ask for the names of more referrals. Many events occur during the course of a year. People change positions. Your clients may have met new people who have a need for your products and services.

J. During your postsale follow-up, remember to use some more subtle reminders about referrals. On your business cards and in your e-mail signatures, remind your clients that you appreciate their referrals. Together with the other steps described in this chapter, those small reminders will be enough for satisfied clients to forward your e-mail or give your business card to a potential client.

A WAY OF LIFE

The bottom line is that getting referrals is just another part of the complete sales process. It should be deeply ingrained in your nature to constantly be on the search for others whose needs you can serve. This is much better than the objective of wait-and-see salespeople, whose goal is to give a good presentation and then see what happens next for the rest of the sales process.

If getting the sale has been your focus, it is time to think bigger. **Each buyer represents the doorway to multiple sales.** Instead of limiting yourself to one sale, consider setting your ultimate objective for each sales appointment as getting referrals that lead to multiple sales. That means providing a sales experience packed with so much value, delivered in such a likable manner, that buyers want to refer you to other people with similar challenges and desires who are in their sphere of influence.

COMING FULL CIRCLE

With active referrals from your buyers, your journey around the Circle of Persuasion is complete. Your next journey around the Circle of Persuasion begins again with the buyer's referral. This time, on the strength of the referral, you begin from a stronger position than with nonreferred potential clients. This is the life of top-performing salespeople, going full circle with buyers beyond closing the sale to the referrals that lead to the next sales appointment.

There is a deep professional satisfaction at being good at what you do. The purpose of this book has been to help you more clearly identify the steps of the sales process and provide hands-on knowledge that enables you to complete that circular journey quickly. May you employ the Circle of Persuasion to exceed all of your sales performance goals and enjoy the fruits of a prosperous sales career.

And now, just to take care of some extra business...

Scenario 1: Business Sales Appointment

Mr. Stevens said *yes* to buying three widgets. Kate is filling in the last of the registration numbers, and the written agreement is ready for his authorization. Her plan is to finish the paperwork and ask Mr. Stevens for referrals. Then Mr. Stevens's intercom beeps. He picks up the phone and listens. With a frown, he turns to Kate and says, "My lunch appointment arrived early. Important clients. What else do we need to do here?"

Kate lays the written agreement on his desk. "Just need your authorization here and down there."

Mr. Stevens pulls the written agreement closer to him and signs his name in the two areas Kate indicated. "Anything else?"

"I'll organize the paperwork and leave a copy with your administrative assistant out front."

"Fine," he says as he stands. "Looking forward to receiving some reliable widgets."

Kate gathers her things. "We appreciate your business. Thank you for your time this morning."

Three months later, Kate stops by Mr. Stevens's office for a routine follow-up call. After greeting him, she announces the purpose of her brief visit. "I wanted to stop by for a moment and make sure those replacement parts got to your team in Canada."

That is Kate's primary reason for stopping by. She also has a second objective of asking Mr. Stevens for referrals, but she knows that the first step in getting referrals is having a happy client. Mr. Stevens is indeed a happy client, and his expression shows his pleasure. "They sure did. I was amazed how quickly you received the parts for a competitor's widget."

"Widget Corp keeps a stocked warehouse for last-minute needs just like this. The tricky part was getting it through customs in time for your team. That was quite an adventure."

"I have experienced that adventure on more than one occasion. Thanks for going the extra mile."

"You're welcome. Is every other aspect of Widget Corp's service meeting or exceeding your expectations?"

"Yes. I'm glad I made the switch."

Kate has quickly re-established rapport and confirmed that Mr. Stevens is content with Widget Corp. Now she is ready to pursue her second reason for stopping by. "You are a valued client. As you might expect, a significant portion of Widget Corp's new business is developed through the referrals of satisfied clients like you. Who are some of your colleagues that are burdened with similar delays caused by aging equipment?"

Kate remains silent, treating her request for referrals like a closing question. In fact, it is. Relaxed and with a pleasant expression on her face, she waits for his reply. Mr. Stevens looks at her blankly as he thinks of possible names. Shifting in his chair, he looks down to one side. Slowly shaking his head, he says, "No names come to mind."

She remains silent a few moments longer and Mr. Stevens continues, "I mean, there are other executives that I meet with quarterly in our professional association. Do you already do business with any of those members?"

Kate encourages his thinking in that direction. "During our first meeting a few months ago, you mentioned working on a project with"—she looks at her notes—"Don Peters. Do you think he is wrestling with some of the same types of delays that you faced before Widget Corp became your service provider?"

"That's a good question. On our last project together, one of his teams might have experienced some problems." With humor, Mr. Stevens tells the story of that team's struggle to stay on schedule with his team.

When he finishes the tale, Kate asks, "You remember how costly those types of delays were for your company? Wouldn't Don appreciate having access to the same type of solutions you had to get your teams' production back to capacity?"

"Probably."

"Who else besides Don do you know in that association who might appreciate access to additional ways to increase their productivity?"

For the next several minutes, Mr. Stevens provides names of several of his colleagues in his professional association. Each name is accompanied by a story about the owner.

Kate writes down each name and then listens to the story without interrupting. When Mr. Stevens stops, Kate quickly confirms the names of the companies his referrals work with. "Thanks so much," she says with sincerity. Kate guesses that Mr. Stevens has the closest business relationship with Don Peters. "When I call each of these businesses, is it all right to let them know how Widget Corp has provided some useful solutions for you?"

"Sure. Tell them Dean Stevens told you to give them a call."

Kate stands. It is the middle of the business day and she

did not announce her visit. She can find the contact information for each company on her own, and as such, she does not want to take any more of Mr. Stevens's time. "As always, we appreciate your business."

By the end of the next business day, Kate has contacted all of the people on the list. She sends a note to Mr. Stevens thanking him again for the referrals and updating him on the names of potential clients with whom she has arranged appointments.

Scenario 2: Residential Sales Appointment

Bob has filled out the written agreement and received the last of the authorizations from Pat and Gary for the purchase of their widget. As he is organizing the paperwork to leave for them, he asks, "As you expressed how relieved you are to finally get this done, I thought about your sister, who you mentioned having a conversation with about widgets. Who are some of the other family, friends, and work associates who are concerned about the potential risks to their families of not having a widget?"

Over the next several minutes, Bob jots down on a blank sheet of paper the names that Pat and sometimes Gary provide. After each name, he asks, "What was it they said or did that brought them to mind just now?" That often leads Pat and Gary to provide one or two more names.

Then Bob asks Pat, "What's the best way to reach your sister?" One by one, he goes through the names they have given him. If they do not readily have the contact information, Bob moves on. Finally he asks, "Since you're so relieved to have the benefits our product will be providing your family, would you mind making a couple of quick calls to let your sister and the Smith family know that you have found a solution to the widget issue, and that it might be helpful to them as well?"

Pat says that she is planning on talking to her sister later that night. She offers to talk with the neighbors across the street the next day. Gary, however, is uncomfortable calling any of his work associates.

"I understand," says Bob. "May I have permission to use your name when I contact them?"

Gary is so relieved to be off the hook on making those calls that he welcomes this suggestion. Bob gathers his things. "Thank you for inviting me into your home this evening. Congratulations on taking action to protect your family in this most important manner."

When Bob walks out to his car, it is dark. Before starting his car, he lowers the windows and listens to the breeze rustling through the trees. He feels drained yet exhilarated, knowing he professionally served the needs of his buyers by successfully journeying with them around the Circle of Persuasion.

Those journeys with potential clients don't always end with a *yes*, but he almost always feels great about the service he renders in helping them make informed decisions that are good for their families. But tonight, the buyers said *yes*... and they gave him the names of several people he will call tomorrow to arrange future appointments. With a sigh, he starts his car, and his thoughts turn to his own family waiting at home.

CHAPTER 18 KEY POINTS

- Referrals from your satisfied buyers are more likely to buy!
- Your job is not finished just because the sale is completed.
- Profit from your buyers' tendency to tell others about finding a solution to their needs.
- Introduce the idea of providing referrals throughout the entire sales appointment.
- Help clients think of who else might have similar needs.
- Ask qualifying questions about the names that were provided.
- Always let clients know the results of contacting their referrals.

CIRCLE OF PERSUASION CHECKLIST

Preparation
Business cards
Pen
Breath mints
Relaxed and focused
Imagine desired response

Establishing Rapport
Smile
Handshake/greeting
Match loudness, pacing
Clearly enunciate words
Match physiology

Identifying Needs
Ask open-ended questions
Listen with physiology
Avoid interruptions
Avoid premature selling
Ask discovery questions

Presentation
Assumptive tone of voice
Match word patterns
Effectively use visual aids
Connect each feature to a benefit
Sell the deeper value

Closing questions
Use trial close questions
Remain relaxed
Remain silent
Ready for *yes, no, maybe*

Inner Circle
Re-establish rapport
Listen with physiology
Find agreement
Clarify question/concern
Confirm there are no other questions
If you answer...then they will buy
Confirm answer is adequate
Close again after answering question
Ask ultimate question

Negotiation
Written list of negotiation points
Know starting and ending points
Remain relaxed when buyer makes request
Clarify buyer's purpose of request
Offer value before reducing price
Commit to action before price reduction
Ask ultimate question before walking

Yes!
Calmly show appreciation
Organized to attend buying details
Aware of buyer's time
Buyer knows what to expect next

Referrals
Foreshadow referral expectations
Re-establish rapport after buying decision
Do not interrupt buyer giving referrals
Get contact info later if time is short
Quickly contact referrals
Follow up with buyer about referrals

Index

About the Authors

Tom Hopkins

The Builder of Sales Champions

Tom Hopkins carries the standard as a master sales trainer and is recognized as the world's leading authority on selling techniques and salesmanship.

More than four million salespeople on five continents have attended Tom's high-energy live seminars. Tom personally conducts more than thirty seminars each year, traveling throughout the United States, Canada, Australia, New Zealand, Singapore, Malaysia, Taiwan, Europe, and the Philippines.

Tom got his start at the young age of nineteen in the field of real estate. After failing miserably his first six months, he discovered that successful selling is a learned skill. He became an avid student, making selling his hobby. By the age of twenty-seven, he achieved millionaire status, having sold more than 1,553 homes.

With his strategies in great demand, Tom moved into the field of training, holding seminars, and creating broadcast-quality video systems and high-quality audio recordings as well as writing books. His proven-effective methods and strategies for selling have been in high demand for nearly forty years.

Tom is the author of *How to Master the Art of Selling*™, which has sold more than 1.6 million copies worldwide. He has also authored sixteen other books on the topics of selling and success.

Ben Katt

Ben's background includes a curious mix of multiple sales formats, speaking, sales training, consulting, and entrepreneurship. His sales experience includes group sales, business to business, residential sales, telephone sales, and art auctioneering. He has spoken in more than one hundred cities in the United States, Canada, Europe, and Australia. He provides sales consulting and organizational behavior consulting for national and regional corporations. Ben and his wife have traveled to more than fifty countries on six continents, climbing the highest mountains on two of those continents.

**BUSINESS
PLUS**

Recognized as one of the world's most prestigious business imprints, Business Plus specializes in publishing books that are on the cutting edge. Like you, to be successful we always strive to be ahead of the curve.

Business Plus titles encompass a wide range of books and interests—including important business management works, state-of-the-art personal financial advice, noteworthy narrative accounts, the latest in sales and marketing advice, individualized career guidance, and autobiographies of the key business leaders of our time.

Our philosophy is that business is truly global in every way, and that today's business reader is looking for books that are both entertaining and educational. To find out more about what we're publishing, please check out the Business Plus blog at:

www.businessplusbooks.com